AMERICAN CITIES CHRONOLOGY SERIES

CLEVELAND
A CHRONOLOGICAL & DOCUMENTARY HISTORY

1760-1976

Compiled and Edited by
ROBERT I. VEXLER

Series Editor
HOWARD B. FURER

1977
OCEANA PUBLICATIONS, INC.
Dobbs Ferry, New York

To my family

Library of Congress Cataloging in Publication Data

Main entry under title:

Cleveland: a chronological & documentary history,
    1760-1976.

    (American cities chronology series)
    Bibliography: p.
    SUMMARY: A chronology of important events in
Cleveland's history accompanied by pertinent documents.
    1. Cleveland — History — Chronology. 2. Cleveland —
History — Sources. [1. Cleveland — History]
I. Vexler, Robert I.
F499.C657C55   977.1'32   77-8946
ISBN 0-379-00604-9

Manufactured in the United States of America

TABLE OF CONTENTS

EDITOR'S FOREWORD

Every effort has been made to cite the most accurate dates in the chronology; various newspapers, documents and letters and chronicles have been consulted to determine the exact date. Later scholarship has been used to verify this information or to change dates when proven plausible.

Because the very nature of preparing a chronology of this type precludes the author from using the standard form of historical footnoting, I should like to acknowledge in this editor's foreword the major sources used to compile the bulk of chronological and factual materials comprising the chronological section of this work: James Harrison Kennedy. <u>A History of the City of Cleveland. Its Settlement, Rise and Progress, 1796-1896</u>; Samuel P. Orth. <u>A History of Cleveland, Ohio with Numerous Chapters by Special Contributors</u>, 3 vols.; William Ganson Rose. <u>Cleveland, the Making of a City</u>; Col. Cha's Whittlesey. <u>Early History of Cleveland, Ohio,...</u>

This research tool is compiled primarily for the student. The importance of political, social, economic and cultural events have been evaluated in relation to their significance for the development of Cleveland as one of the major cities that have contributed to the growth of America. Cleveland has contributed much to the growth and development of the United States. Its citizens recognized the importance and made use of its strategic location on Lake Erie. They made use of their position to begin to play a major role in the industrial and commercial development of the nation. Cleveland recognized the importance of urban reconstruction especially after the end of the Second World War, and set to work to redevelop her central core and downtown area.

Documents have been selected, which best illustrate the major aspects in the development of Cleveland from the small early American town to the fast developing city of the postwar era.

Robert I. Vexler
Briarcliff College

EARLY DEVELOPMENT OF CLEVELAND

1760   November 7. Major Robert Rogers and his British troops reached the mouth of the Cuyahoga River, site of Cleveland. Soon thereafter, they met a party of Indian chiefs proclaiming they were an embassy from Pontiac.

1787   With the issuance of the Ordinance of 1787, it may be said that practical civil government was established throughout Ohio.

October 5. Congress elected Major General Arthur St. Clair of Pennsylvania the first governor of the northwest territory.

1796   July 22. Moses Cleaveland arrived at the mouth of the Cuyahoga River with the first company of Connecticut settlers, and founded the town.

September 22. The first survey of Cleveland was begun. It was completed October 17, and the surveyors left on October 18.

September 30. Moses Cleaveland left the town bearing his name and never returned.

1797   Major Alonzo Carter's cabin was the first public house to be built.

Edward Paine opened the first dry goods store.

January 23. Charles Phelps Stiles was the first child born in Cleveland. He was the son of Job Phelps and Tabitha Stiles.

June 1. Reverend Seth Hart led the second company of settlers of the Connecticut Company to the town. He held the first religious services, a funeral for Alonzo Carter, who was drowned.

July 4. Chloe Inches, Mrs. Lorenzo Carter's helper, married William Clement. This was the first wedding in the town.

1798   Samuel Dodge, the first carpenter, arrived in Cleveland.

January 30. A committee of the Connecticut Company recommended cutting a road from Pennsylvania to Cleveland.

1799   January. Nathan Doan built a tavern.

June. David Hudson founded the settlement of Hudson which was incorporated as a village in 1837.

1800   Rev. Joseph Badger preached the first sermon for Baptists.

Axtell Street Cemetery was opened.

David Bryant arrived and built a distillery.

July 10. Governor St. Clair created Trumbull County which included the entire Western Reserve. A proclamation was issued ordering that elections be held on the second Tuesday of October to select on representative for the territorial legislature.

August 25. The first court of quarter sessions in Trumbull County was held. The County was divided into eight townships, including Cleveland, which included all of Cuyahoga County east of the river, and other townships in Geauga County.

1801   Major Lorenzo Carter was given a license to keep a tavern.

July 4. The first grand ball was held in Cleveland.

August 18. Rev. Joseph Badger of Connecticut visited Cleveland.

1802   April 5. The inhabitants of Cleveland held an election at the house of James Kingsbury, Esq. Rodolphus Edwards was chosen Chairman, and Nathaniel Doan, town clerk.

September. Rev. Joseph Badger organized the first Congregational Church at Hudson. He had earlier preached the first sermons at Cleveland.

November 1. The first state constitutional convention met at Chillicothe, and completed and ratified a constitution within thirty days.

1803   A mail route was established from Warren
            through various towns to Cleveland.

            February 19. Congress declared the eastern
            portion of the Northwest Territory, south of
            Lake Erie, the state of Ohio.

            Spring. At the township elections, Amos
            Spofford was elected Chairman, and Nathaniel
            Doan, town clerk.

            October 11. The first election under the
            Ohio constitution was held in Cleveland to
            select representatives to the legislature.

1804   April. A town tax of $10 was ordered at the
            town meeting.

            May 7. The Fourth Militia Company elected
            Lorenzo Carter Captain in its first election.

1805   April. Elisha Norton became the first post-
            master of the town.

            July 4. The final treaty of purchase of
            Cleveland from the Indians was arranged.

1806   October. Asael Adams began a private school.
            He was to earn $10 per month.

1807   Amos Spofford opened a tavern, which became
            the Wallace House, and eventually The Man-
            sion House, which was then destroyed by fire
            in 1835.

            November 16. Moses Cleaveland died, and was
            buried in Canterbury, Connecticut.

1808   Alonzo Carter built the first ship in Cleve-
            land, the Zephyr.

            The Cleveland-Erie mail route was set up with
            John Metcalf as carrier.

1809   A mail route was opened to Detroit.

1810   May 1. The Cuyahoga County government was
            begun. Benjamin Ruggles was selected pre-
            siding judge.

            June. The first resident doctor, David Long,
            arrived. He participated in many affairs in
            the city. He died September 1, 1851.

June 5. The Court of Common Pleas held its first session.

1811   August 23. The Free Masons were organized at a meeting in Harvey Murray's house. Lewis Cass, grand master of Ohio, gave the dispensation.

1812   George Wallace opened a tavern on Superior Street.

Construction of the County courthouse and jail was begun on Public Square. The building was completed in 1813. It was torn down in 1830.

June 24. The first execution in Cleveland was that of the Indian John O'Mic, who murdered two trappers.

June 28. News of the outbreak of war with Great Britain on June 18 reached the village.

1813   General of the Army William Henry Harrison visited Cleveland.

May 10. Captain Stanton Stoles and his troops arrived at Carter's Tavern. They built Fort Huntington and a small hospital.

September 10. The battle of Lake Erie was fought and won by Commodore Oliver Perry.

CLEVELAND AS A VILLAGE

1814   December 23. Cleveland received its Charter. The electors were to meet the first Monday in June, 1815, to elect its officers.

1815   May. Mowry's Tavern was built. It was enlarged several times. In 1852 William A. Smith bought the property and named it the Forest City House.

June 5. Elections were held in which Alfred Kelley was selected President, and served until his resignation on March 19, 1816.

June 13. George Wallace purchased Spofford's Tavern, renaming it the Wallace House.

October 15. Newburgh Township was organized.

1816   Some citizens subscribed $200 to build a
            school house.

            The Cleveland Pier Company was chartered to
            build a wharf on Lake Erie.

            March 19. Alfred Kelley resigned as the
            village's first President. He was succeeded
            by his father Daniel, who was elected in June
            at the annual meeting, and continued in of-
            fice until 1819.

            August 6. The Commercial Bank of Lake Erie
            opened with Alfred Kelley as President. It
            failed in 1820, and was reorganized April 2,
            1832. When its charter expired in 1842, the
            legislature would not renew it. T. P. Hardy
            was appointed trustee, and distributed the
            remaining assets to the stockholders in
            June, 1845.

            November 9. Trinity Episcopal Parish was or-
            ganized in Phineas Shepherd's house.

1817   The Archwood Presbyterian Church was organ-
            ized.

            January 13. The village trustees voted to
            assume control over the new school house on
            St. Clair Street, and to refund the money to
            the subscribers.

1818   June 1. Brooklyn Township was organized.

            July 31. The first issue of The Cleaveland
            Gazette and Commercial Register appeared. It
            continued until March 21, 1820.

            August 11. The Gazette announced the begin-
            ning of a mail stage between Cleveland and
            Painesville.

            August 25. The steamboat Walk-in-the-Water
            arrived in Cleveland.

1819   September. Bishop Philander Chase made the
            first Episcopal visitation to Trinity Parish.
            He confirmed ten persons.

            October 19. The first edition of the Cleave-
            land Herald appeared, edited by Eber D. Howe.
            It became a daily in 1835. Whittlesey and
            Harris purchased the Gazette and the Herald

in 1837.

1820   The population was 606.

A stage line was established to Columbus and
Norwalk, and then to Pittsburgh.

Independence Road was opened to Akron.

February 23. The Legislature authorized appointment of three commissioners to locate
a route for a canal between Lake Erie and the
Ohio River.

May 23. The first theatrical entertainment
was given in Mowrey's Tavern by Blanchard's
traveling company.

June. Horace Perry was elected President
of the village.

August. The trustees passed legislation to
clean up the village.

September 19. The Old Stone Church was organized by the Congregationalists. It was
to be the mother of Presbyterian churches in
Cleveland.

1821   The Old Brick Academy on St. Clair Street
was completed. It was the first private
school.

April 27. Ulysses S. Grant was born at Point
Pleasant on the Ohio River.

June. Leonard Case was elected President of
the village, and continued to be elected annually until 1825. He refused to qualify in
the last year.

1822   June 26. The Cleveland Academy opened under
Rev. William McLean.

1823   Job Doan and others formed a society to buy
a cemetery.

March 29. The Cuyahoga County Agricultural
Society was established at the Court House.

1824   David Hudson donated $2,142 and 160 acres of
land for the future home of Western Reserve
College, later Adelbert College.

Elijah Ingersol started a singing school for the winter evenings.

May. The physicians and surgeons of the 19th district were organized.

The Navy Hotel was opened.

1825   February 24. Cleveland was chosen as the northern terminus of the Ohio Canal, in the Ohio Canal Act.

March 3. The Federal Government appropriated $5,000 to construct a pier at the mouth of the River.

June. Leonard Case failed to qualify upon his election as President. The recorder Eleazer Waterman became president ex-officio. He probably continued to fill both offices until 1828, although the records are not clear.

September 29-October 1. The first circus was held in Cleveland.

October 26. The Erie Canal was opened.

1826   Rev. Freeman opened a school for ladies.

The county commissioners decided to build a new courthouse. It was finally decided that the county seat ought to be situated at Cleveland, rather than Newburgh.

Philo Scovill built the Franklin House, named after Benjamin Franklin.

The village secured land for a cemetery on Erie Street.

February 7. The Presbyterians received a charter to establish a new literary and theo-logical institution at Hudson. The college opened in the Fall of 1827.

April. A new stage began running twice a week between Pittsburgh and Cleveland.

Fall. Rev. Thomas Martin, a Dominican, came to Cleveland to serve the Catholics.

October 28. The first court was held in the

new courthouse.

1827   Rev. John Crawford formed the pioneering
                class of the first Methodist Episcopal
                Church.

                The Whigs established the daily paper The
                Advertiser.

                The Cuyahoga County Colonization Society was
                formed as a branch of the National Coloniza-
                tion Society, with Samuel Cowles as presi-
                dent. Its aim was to help freed blacks to
                leave the country.

                January 5. The first Presbyterian Society
                was incorporated.

                July 4. The first boat arrived in Cleveland
                on the Erie Canal.

                July 21. The first issue of the Western In-
                telligencer, a religious weekly appeared,
                with Harmon Kingsbury and Rev. Randolph
                Stone as editors.

                Summer. A typhoid fever epidemic broke out.

1828   Mrs. Sally Mather Hale began a Sunday School
                in her home.

                The Twinsbury Literary Institute was formed
                as a college preparatory school.

                E. Waterman was elected President and Recor-
                der. He had to resign May 30 because of ill
                health. The Trustees appointed Oirson Cathan
                President, and E. H. Beardsley Recorder.

                October 28. The first court session was held
                in the new two-story brick Court House.

1829   Noah D. Haskell and J. C. Hall kept school.

                Cleveland had its first light house.

                A hand fire engine, the first in the village,
                was brought to Cleveland.

                April. Dr. David Long, Cleveland's first
                physician, was elected President.

                August 12. Bishop Chase consecrated Trinity

Parish Church.

1830 Richard Hilliard was elected President of the village, and was reelected in 1831.

A regular fire company was formed, and a new engine purchased for it, called Eagle No. 1.

A free school was formed, supported by sub-scription, for the education of all children.

St. John's African Methodist Episcopal Church, first Negro religious group in Cleve-land, was formed.

March 31. The temperance movement was begun at a meeting in the courthouse.

July 10. Navigation began on the Ohio Canal from Lake Erie to Newark, which brought much business to Cleveland.

1831 January 6. The first issue of the <u>Cleveland Advertiser</u> appeared. It was a weekly pub-lished by Henry Bolles and Madison Kelley. It became a daily in 1836, and finally a morning paper, with an afternoon edition, in 1885.

November 19. James A. Garfield was born in a log cabin in Cuyahoga County.

1832 The first boat travelled the entire length of the Ohio Canal.

Asiatic cholera reached Cleveland.

John W. Allen was elected President, and continued in office until 1835.

June 24. The village trustees appointed the first board of health under Dr. David Long.

1833 The first formal dancing academy was opened.

William Cook built the first theater.

J. H. Black opened a classical school in the Brick Academy.

Miss Ward opened a young ladies' school in the Academy.

The Cleveland Anti-Slavery Society was organized with Dr. David Long as President.

January 25. The Legislature granted a charter to Philo Scovill and others to organize the Cleveland Water Company to serve Cleveland and Cuyahoga County.

February. The Cleveland Lyceum was incorporated.

The Legislature passed an act to encourage the organization of fire companies. Forty-five volunteers formed the Live Oak Company in Cleveland in 1834.

February 16. The First Baptist Church was organized.

April 22. The Erie & Kalamazoo Railway Company was chartered. It was the first section of The Lake Shore and Michigan Southern Railroad. The Michigan Southern Railway, chartered May 9, 1846, bought the bankrupt Erie & Kalamazoo in May, 1849.

August 20. Benjamin Harrison, who was to be the 23rd President of the United States, was born at North Bend, Ohio.

1834 The Bank of Cleveland was organized with a capital of $300,000, under Norman C. Baldwin as president.

January 20. The first serious fire occurred in the village.

March 3. The Cleveland and Newburgh Railroad Company was incorporated.

June 2. John W. Allen was elected President of the village.

August 20. L. L. Rice started the _Cleveland Whig_. The paper was sold to Whittlesey and Lewis December 17, 1836.

October. The journeymen printers formed the Cleveland Typographical Association.

November 3. A medical college was opened in connection with Willoughby University.

1835   The Cleveland Reading Room Association was organized with John M. Sterling, president.

The Cleveland Harmonic Society was formed.

Dr. Benjamin Strickland was the first dentist in Cleveland.

June 2. John W. Allen was reelected President of Cleveland.

THE CITY OF CLEVELAND

1836   William R. Richardson opened Spring Cottage, a small hotel on the lake.

Free schools were established.

March 5. The Legislature passed an act incorporating the City of Cleveland.

March 14. A charter was granted to the Cleveland, Columbus & Cincinnati Railroad.

The Cleveland & Pittsburgh Railroad was chartered as The Cleveland, Warren & Pittsburgh Railroad. The final connection with Pittsburgh was made in 1852.

March 15. The Cleveland City Temperance Society was organized.

March 29. Joseph Barber was elected Mayor under the new City Charter.

April 11. John W. Willey was elected Mayor. He was reelected in 1837.

April 15. The City Council held its first meeting.

April 25. The Ohio Railroad Company was organized in Painesville.

May. L. L. Rice started the _Daily Gazette_. It was sold to Whittlesey and Lewis on January 1, 1837. It was combined with the _Herald_ in the Spring of 1837, as the _Herald and Gazette_. Its name was changed to the _Herald_ in 1843.

May 17. The Council passed an ordinance which

regulated the newly created Fire Department.

June 22. A school levy was authorized, making it possible to open the first public school.

October 5. The Council appointed the first board of school managers: John W. Willey, Anson Hayden and Daniel Worley.

November. The Young Men's Literary Association was formed.

1837   Jonathan Fowler opened the Commercial Hotel.

Julius P. McCabe issued the <u>Directory--Cleveland and Ohio City, for the Years 1837-38</u>.

Misses E. Johnston and Hollison opened a young ladies' school.

February 22. The Cleveland City Guards, a private military company, was organized.

April. The Cleveland Female Orphan Asylum was incorporated.

July 4. The Cuyahoga Anti-Slavery Society was formed with Edward Wade as President.

July 7. The Council finally passed an ordinance establishing a school system.

August 14. The American House, the first large hotel in the city, opened.

October 27. Mayor Willey sent the militia guard to the Columbus Street Bridge, because of trouble with Ohio City over the use of the bridge.

1838   January 11. A County Association for the furtherance of common school education was established with John W. Willey as president.

March. Joshua Mills was elected Mayor, and then was reelected in 1839.

March 5. Brighton was incorporated as a village.

March 6. By vote of the Council, Marshal Kirk was to retain two per cent of all fees collected.

March 21. The citizens of Cleveland met and
drafted resolutions against the national
sub-treasury plan.

August 30. The trustees of Shaw Academy were
elected in accordance with the will of John
Shaw.

1839   The Israelitic Society, first permanent Jew-
            ish religious organization, was estanlished.
            They purchased a burial ground in Ohio City
            for $100. In 1842 a division occurred, and
            the seceders formed the Anshe Chesed Society.

            The Colored Men's Union Society was formed.

            The city built a small Market house, and ap-
            pointed L. D. Johnson market clerk.

            The firemen organized a Mutual Protection
            Society for aiding firemen injured at fires.

            March. Joshua Mills was reelected Mayor.

1840   J. W. Watson built the Globe Theater.

            Miss Butler founded a school for children
            aged three to eight.

            March 2. Nicholas Dockstader was elected
            Mayor.

            March 7. The Westside Whigs organized the
            Tippecanoe Club of Ohio City.

            April 4. The Cleveland Whigs established
            the Tippecanoe Club of Cuyahoga County.

            June 13. William Henry Harrison visited
            Cleveland during his Presidential campaign.

1841   March 1. John W. Allen was elected Mayor.

            November 12. The twelve-acre Monroe Cemetery
            was opened.

1842   Cleveland Lodge No. 13 of the Odd Fellows was
            organized.

            E. B. Fisher began publication of the weekly
            Cleveland Gatherer, which continued until

1844.

January 7. The _Plain Dealer_ was first issued.

April 12. The Buffalo and Erie development of the Lake Shore & Michigan Southern Railroad was begun.

April 25. Charles Dickens arrived in Cleveland.

1843

January 29. William McKinley was born at Nile, Ohio.

March. Nelson Hayward was elected Mayor.

April 22. The _Emigrant_, the first Cleveland-built steam propeller ship, was launched.

August 4. The Cleveland Medical College was organized, when the Trustees of Western Reserve voted to have six physicians establish a committee to present names of candidates for the M.D. degree.

1844

R. B. Dennis began publication of _The Ohio American_ in Ohio City. This was the origin of _The Cleveland Leader_. It merged with the _True Democrat_ in 1848, and then _The Leader_.

1845

A new Cleveland Library Association was formed.

Miss Thayer opened the Female Seminary on Prospect Street.

The Canal Bank of Cleveland was organized with a capital of $200,000, and E. F. Gaylord as president.

March 3. Samuel Starkweather was reelected Mayor.

March 10. A local branch of the Erie Railroad was begun, when the Franklin & Warren Railroad was chartered. A road was built from the Pennsylvania line to Dayton through Warren, Akron and Springfield. It was called the Atlantic & Great Western in 1854. The Pennsylvania connection was made in April 1858; the Atlantic & Great Western Railroad of Pennsylvania was incorporated in December,

1858, and a connection was made with New York. Various state corporations were consolidated August 19, 1865. Later, the line was leased to the Erie Railroad.

April 7. The _Plain Dealer_ was issued as an evening paper.

May 17. The City Bank of Cleveland was incorporated when the Firemen's Insurance Company was given the power to become involved in general banking. It opened July 1. It closed February 12, 1865, reopening February 13 as The National City Bank of Cleveland. The first president was Reuben Sheldon, and the capital was $200,000.

June 25. The Merchants Bank, first branch of the State Bank to be organized in Cleveland, was chartered for twenty years, with P. M. Weddell as president, and a capital of $112,500.

August. Moses C. Younglove bought the first steam printing press to Cleveland.

September. Peter Baxter started the _Cleveland Weekly Times_, with Horace Steele as editor. It was purchased by the _Plain Dealer_ in 1848.

The Commercial Branch Bank of the State Bank was organized with William A. Otis as president, and a capital of $162,500. When its charter expired March 1, 1865, its business was assumed by The Commercial National Bank.

September 10. H. Steele and P. Baxter issued _The Cleveland Times_, a weekly.

November 24. The first meeting of the Cleveland Academy of Natural Science was held, with Dr. Jared P. Kirtland elected as its president.

1846   The _Germania_ became the first German newspaper published in Cleveland.

E. S. Hamlin founded the _True Democrat_, a weekly anti-slavery Whig paper, which was first issued at Olmsted Falls, and then moved to Cleveland on September 1, where it absorbed _The American_.

January.   The Cleveland Medical Lyceum was
organized by the faculty and students of
Cleveland Medical College.

March 2.   George Hoadley was elected Mayor.

May 5.   The St. Andrews Society was organized
to aid Scottish immigrants.

May 15.   The Israelitic and Anshe Chesed Societies were reunited, but the groups split
again in 1848.

1846   June 22.   The Cleveland Board of Underwriters
was formed with Joseph L. Weatherly as president.

1847   The township of East Cleveland was organized.

The Superior Court of Cleveland was created.

January.   Dr. Horace A. Ackley amputated a
leg with the patient under full anesthesia,
with ether, in the Medical Department of
Western Reserve College.

January 13.   E. S. Hamlin and E. L. Stevens
issued the Daily True Democrat as a morning
paper dedicated to abolition.   It was consolidated with The Forest City in 1853, and
was later absorbed by the Leader.

February 11.   Thomas Alva Edison was born
at Milan, Ohio.

March.   Joseph A. Harris was elected Mayor.

Spring.   A class for girls was established in
the high school.

April 23.   The Diocese of Cleveland was
created.

May.   The New England Hotel was opened.   It
was destroyed by fire in 1856.

June 25.   The Weddell House was opened.

October 10.   Rev. Amadeus Rappe was consecrated Catholic Bishop of Cleveland.

1848   The Lake Telegraph Company was chartered,
operating from Buffalo to Cleveland.

Union College, the first branch of the Bryant
and Stratton business college chain, was
founded.

The Cuyahoga County Homeopathic Society was
organized.

Wick, Otis & Brownell, a private banking
firm, was founded.

The Cleveland Academy was opened for the
education of young ladies.

An English and Classical School for boys was
established.

The High School pupils began editing The
School Boy.

February. The Cleveland Library Association
was incorporated.

The Cleveland, Painesville & Ashtabula Railroad was chartered to be built to the Penn-
sylvania-Ohio border. In May, 1854, the
Pennsylvania Legislature gave authority to
extend the road to Erie, where it connected
with the Erie & Northeast Railway.

February 22. The Cleveland & Mahoning Valley
Railroad Company was chartered. It was
leased to the Atlantic & Great Western Railroad in October, 1863.

March 6. Captain Lorenzo A. Kelsey was elected Mayor.

July 7. The merchants formed the Board of
Trade at the Weddell House, with Joseph L.
Weatherly as president. After a period of
inactivity, it was revitalized in 1866, and
the reorganized in February, 1893 as the
Chamber of Commerce.

August 14. John S. Potter's theater opened
on Water Street.

October. Linda T. Guilford opened the Young
Ladies Seminary.

1849   The Legislature authorized the City Council
to establish a poor house and hospital for
the poor.

The barge <u>Eureka</u>, under Captain William
Monroe, sailed for the California gold
fields.

March. The Cleveland Mutual Fire Insurance
Company was incorporated.

March 5. Flavel W. Bingham was elected
Mayor.

March 22. The Society for Savings was chartered as a mutual society, with John W. Allen
as president.

June 26. The first case of cholera was diag-
nosed, and the second epidemic began.

October. The Buffalo & State Line Railroad
was organized to build west from Buffalo,
and to connect with a road leading to Cleveland. The road was permitted to join with
the Erie & Northeast to be known as the Buffalo & Erie Company.

November 3. The first locomotive was seen
in Cleveland.

1850   The population was 17,034.

<u>The Spirit of the Lakes</u> was issued by the
Western Seamen's Friend Society, Rev. R. H.
Leonard, editor. It became <u>The Spirit of
the Lakes and Boatmen's Reporter</u> in 1853.

Hecker's Band was the first important one
in the city.

The City Infirmary was begun, and finally
completed in 1855.

The Detroit & Cleveland Navigation Company
was begun to run boats between Detroit and
Cleveland. It was incorporated in Michigan
in 1868.

January 3. <u>The Family Visitor</u>, a weekly, was
first issued.

March. The State Legislature passed a law
establishing the Cleveland College of Homeo-
pathy.

March 4. William Case was elected Mayor,

and reelected in 1851.

March 9. The Carroll County Railroad Company was chartered. It was sold to the Ohio & Toledo Railroad Company in 1873, and reorganized as the Cleveland & Canton Railroad Company on June 24, 1875. It was then sold to the newly organized Coshocton & Southern Railroad. Finally, in May, 1892, the railroads were consolidated as the Cleveland, Canton and Southern Railroad.

May 26. The Tifereth Israel Congregation was formed as a result of dissension in the Anshe Chesed Organization.

June 27. The Cleveland Ladies Temperance Union was organized.

September 10. Judge Hitchcock and Dr. Aiken addressed a large meeting at Empire Hall to denounce the fugitive slave act.

October. Cleveland University was founded.

October 8. Cleveland Democrat Reuben Wood was elected Governor of Ohio.

1851   The Young Men's Christian Association was begun as a result of informal prayers by a group of young men.

Bishop Rappe established two orphan asylums: St. Vincent's for boys and St. Mary's for girls.

The Union Steamboat Company, one of the first freight transportation lines, was begun.

February 18. Alfred Kelley and Mayor William Case drove the last spikes in the Cleveland, Columbus & Cincinnati Railroad.

February 19. The charter of the Cleveland, Mt. Vernon & Delaware Railroad was issued to the Cleveland & Pittsburgh Railroad Company to build the Akron branch. The line was finally controlled by the Pennsylvania Railroad in 1869.

February 22. A banquet was held celebrating the opening of Cleveland's first railway, the Cleveland, Columbus & Cincinnati.

March 18. Cleveland University was incorporated. It was discontinued in 1854. Then in 1856, Professor R. E. Humiston organized a company, and took over the property to develop the Cleveland Institute.

April 7. William Case was reelected Mayor.

May. The Commercial Mutual Insurance Company was organized. Its officers were elected May 21.

August 19. The American Association for the Advancement of Education opened a four-day convention in Cleveland.

October 14. The residents of Cleveland voted against a proposed merger with Ohio City.

November 6. Jenny Lind first came to Cleveland, and sang at Kelley's Hall on November 7.

December 9. The Mercantile Library Association was organized.

1852   The city purchased sixty acres from Benjamin Butler for $13,639.50, and established Woodland Cemetery.

Joseph and James C. Medill established The Daily Forest City. Competition with the True Democrat led to a merger of the two. In March, 1854, the paper was renamed The Leader. In 1861, an afternoon edition called the Evening Leader was published, which was changed to the Evening News in 1868. When the Herald was bought, the paper was called the News and Herald. The first Sunday edition appeared in 1872.

The Marine Hospital was opened. Construction had begun in 1847. In 1875, the Hospital was leased to the city on condition that certain wards be reserved for government use. The City Hospital Association gave up the building in 1896, when the Marine Hospital Service resumed control.

January 22. The Cleveland Orphan Asylum was begun by Mrs. Benjamin Rouse and members of the Dorcas Society.

April 5. Abner C. Brownell was elected Mayor, the last selected under the old charter. He was reelected in 1853.

May 3. The Ohio Legislature passed an act incorporating cities and villages. It divided cities into first class (over 200,000), and second class (all others).

August 2. The first number of Der Waechter am Erie appeared. It changed from a semi-weekly to a tri-weekly, and then a daily on September 17, 1866.

September 15-17. The Ohio State Fair was held in Cleveland for the first time.

November. The first locomotive traveled the entire length of the Cleveland, Painesville & Ashtabula Railroad.

1853   The Division Street Bridge was built.

The Lake Superior Line between Cleveland and the Sault was organized.

The competing telegraph lines serving Cleveland, Buffalo, Milwaukee, Columbus, Cincinnati, St. Louis, Wheeling, Zanesville, Warren and Pittsburgh merged as the Speed and Wade Telegraph lines.

April. William Howard Day edited and published the first Negro newspaper, The Aliened American. He published another paper in August.

The first Board of Water Works Commissioners was elected.

April 4. Mayor Brownell was reelected.

April 16. The Cleveland Theater opened.

April 17. The first session of the Cleveland Police Court, authorized by the Legislature, was held.

June 1. The Council established a Board of Education, with power to appoint a Superintendent of Instruction.

June 14. Woodland Cemetery was dedicated.

October 5. The National Woman' Rights Convention opened a three-day session at Melodeon Hall.

CLEVELAND ENLARGED: MERGER WITH OHIO CITY

1854   February 1. Cleveland's first fancy dress
ball was held in Ballou's Hall.

February 6. Rev. Samuel C. Aiken presided
over the organizational meeting of the Young
Men's Christian Association.

April 2. Cleveland and Ohio City residents
voted to merge. The enlarged City Council
met June 10.

April 17. The Angier House, a fashionable
Hotel, opened.

May 20. The Cleveland Female Seminary, organized by Rev. E. M. Sawtelle, opened.

November 2. The Herald and the Plain Dealer
contracted with the Associated Press to receive telegraphic reports of news.

November 13. R. B. Wheeler and E. A. Payne
founded the Cleveland Academy of Music.

1855   A three-day Saengerfest, the first music
festival in Cleveland, was held under the
leadership of Hans Balatka of Milwaukee.

February 7. The Northern Indiana Railroad
Company was formed through a consolidation
of the western division of the Buffalo &
Mississippi, the Northern Indiana, and the
Northern Indiana and Chicago Railroads.

April 2. William B. Castle, People's Party
candidate, was elected Mayor.

August. John D. Rockefeller graduated from
Folson's Mercantile College.

October 17. The first American Rabbinical
Conference met at Cleveland.

December. The New England Society of Cleveland was organized with Benjamin Rouse as
president.

December 14. The Tifereth Israel Congregation Temple was dedicated.

1856   January 10. An ordinance creating a Board of Health was passed, beginning the sanitary system. A new Board of Health was created in 1859.

April 1. Central High School was dedicated.

April 4. The Western Union Telegraph Company was created through consolidation of thirteen telegraph companies.

May. A Kansas Emigration Society was established, with Charles Hickox as president, to raise funds.

Dr. S. R. Beckwith organized the first privately owned hospital in Cleveland: the Cleveland Homeopathic Hospital.

August. The City and State Board of Public Works authorized the construction of the Willow Street Bridge. This bridge was replaced in 1896 by an electrically operated drawbridge.

September 14. Cleveland's first central pumping station, the Kentucky Street Reservoir, was opened.

1857   The Euclid City Station Line, a street car line, was opened.

January 29. Ralph Waldo Emerson lectured at Melodeon Hall on "The Conduct of Life."

April. Samuel Starkweather was elected Mayor.

August 25. A national emancipation convention, meeting at Melodeon Hall, recommended compensated emancipation.

August 29. H. M. Johnson began the first penny paper in Cleveland, The Daily Review, which continued until 1861.

November 3. The Northern Ohio Dental Association was formed.

November 10. The County Commissioners signed a contract with George P. Smith and James

Pannell for construction of a new courthouse, now known as the "old courthouse."

1858   The Burnett House was opened in the market district. It was refurbished in 1867, and opened as the Cleveland Hotel.

February. The Cuyahoga County Historical Society was established.

April 18. The Sunday Morning Review appeared as the first Sunday paper.

July. The Cleveland Monthly Review was first published, continuing until 1861.

November 8. The Cleveland Chess Club was organized with Leonard Case, Jr. as president.

December 28. The Clearing House Association was established to facilitate daily exchange between member banks and bankers.

December 29. The new Government building on Public Sqaure, housing the Post Office, Custom House, and federal courts and offices was opened.

1859   William Case began construction of a building for the Young Men's Library Association, and the Kirtland Society of Natural History.

March 18. John D. Rockefeller and Maurice B. Clark opened a produce commission business.

April. The Cuyahoga County Medical Society was organized as a successor of the Nineteenth Medical District of Ohio, with Dr. C. A. Terry as president.

April 4. George B. Senter was elected Mayor.

The new Board of Education with a member from each board, as stipulated by the State Legislature, was elected. It proved too large and clumsy.

April 7. The trial of Simeon Bushnell, one of a group of men who rescued a fugitive slave called John from Anderson Jennings, an agent of John G. Bacon of Kentucky, began.

The trial drew national attention. Bushnell
was found guilty of rescuing a fugitive from
service, and was sentenced to a fine of $600
or 60 days' imprisonment in the county jail.

October 25. The Kinsman Street Railroad
Company received a twenty-year charter.

1860   The Town Hall was built on the square called
Miles Park.

August 6. Harry S. Steevens, president of
the East Cleveland Railway Company, broke
ground for the first street railway to operate continuously.

September 10. Commodore Perry's Statue was
the first monument erected on Public Square.

1861   January 19. Deputy U. S. Marshal Seth A.
Abby led a possee of federal officers into
the home of L. A. Benton, and took away a
mulatto girl, Lucy, supposedly a runaway
slave belonging to William S. Goshorn of
Wheeling, Virginia. Judge Tilden ordered her
release on January 21, because a county officer had no right to hold her. The U. S.
Marshal took her into custody. On January
23, Judge Spaulding ruled that she should be
returned. An attempt was made to release her
on the way to Virginia, but it failed.

February 15. President-elect Abraham Lincoln
was welcomed when his train arrived in Cleveland.

April 1. Edward S. Flint was elected Mayor.

April 16. The Cleveland Grays were mustered
into service at the beginning of the Civil
War as Company D, the first Ohio Volunteer
Infantry.

April 25. The Ladies Aid Society was organized to help in the war effort.

October 1. The first draft for war service
had to be held in three wards. The others
had raised their quotas.

1862   August. C. G. Bruce began publication of
The Soldiers Journal.

September 10. Governor David Tod appealed
to the Ohio cities to mobilize volunteer
defenses.

December 17. The first steam fire engine
was purchased for the city.

1863   The Center Street wooden drawbridge was
built. When it became unsafe in 1871, plans
were made to replace it with an iron bridge.

Dr. Gustav C. E. Weber, Professor of Surgery
of Cleveland Medical College, organized the
Charity Hospital Medical College. It was
affiliated with the University of Wooster in
1869. In 1896, the medical college severed
its connection with the University of Wooster,
and formed the Cleveland College of Physicians
and Surgeons, which became affiliated with
Ohio Wesleyan University.

February 2. The volunteer fire department
was abandoned.

February 10. The West Side Street Railway
Company was given its first grant. Ground
was broken on February 16.

March 31. The Union League was organized.

April. An ordinance was passed establishing
a paid steam fire department.

April 6. Irvine U. Masters was elected Mayor.

May 23. The First National Bank was formed,
and took over the business of the private
banking house of S. W. Chittenden & Company
under George W. Worthington as president.

June 9. The St. Clair Street Railroad Company was granted its first charter for twenty
years.

November 3. The first train arrived in Cleveland from New York City on the Atlantic &
Great Western Railroad.

1864   May. Mayor Masters resigned because of ill
health. The Council selected George B. Senter to replace him.

May 19. A Non-Importation League was organized. Its report of May 30, urged people to live economically, and not to purchase foreign goods.

May 31. The Fremont Convention, consisting of anti-Lincoln men, met. They nominated General Fremont for President.

August. An alarm telegraph system was installed in Cleveland, with signal boxes on posts, near the sidewalks throughout the business district.

December 1. The Commercial National Bank was organized, taking over the business of the Commercial Branch Bank, when its charter expired March 1, 1865. Its twenty-year charter was renewed in 1884. William A. Otis was president.

December 27. The Merchants National Bank was organized, beginning business on February 27, 1865, when it absorbed the Merchants Bank. When its charter expired in December, 1884, its successor, the Mercantile National Bank, was organized.

1865   The Metropolitan Police Act created a Board of Police Commissioners, consisting of the Mayor and four others.

The Anchor Line, the Erie & Western Transportation Company, was organized. Its passenger boats stopped in Cleveland.

February 12. The City Bank received a national bank charter, opening February 13 as the National City Bank of Cleveland.

April 3. Henry M. Chapin was elected Mayor.

April 28. The funeral procession of Abraham Lincoln arrived in Cleveland.

August. The Charity Hospital was opened to the public.

October 21. The first baseball match game in Cleveland was played. The Penfield Club of Oberlin defeated the Forest City Nine, 67-28. The Forest City Club was the first amateur club.

CLEVELAND IN THE POST CIVIL WAR ERA

1866   April 3. The Legislature passed an act au-
            thorizing the incorporation of Boards of
            Trade and Chambers of Commerce. The Cleve-
            land Board met and signed the incorporation
            papers on April 5.

            May 1. J. W. Frazee was appointed first su-
            perintendent of Police.

            May 14. The first sleeping coach was seen
            in Cleveland, on the Cleveland and Toledo
            Railroad.

            June 14. The Angier House had been remodeled,
            and reopened as the Kennard House.

            September 3. President Andrew Johnson vi-
            sited Cleveland.

            December 11. The Cleveland Post of the Grand
            Army of the Republic held its first regular
            meeting.

1867   Dr. John Dickinson was appointed first po-
            lice surgeon.

            Charles Whittlesey's _Early History of Cleve-
            land_ was published.

            January. _The Ohio Medical and Surgical Re-
            porter_, a bimonthly, was first issued and
            continued until 1876.

            January 22. Lake View Park, the first park
            purchased by the city, was created.

            February 27. Portions of Brooklyn and New-
            burg townships were annexed to Cleveland.

            March 24. One hundred German immigrants
            formed the Socialer Turn-Verein.

            April 1. Stephen Buhner was elected Mayor.

            April 11. The organizational meeting of the
            Western Reserve Historical Society was held.
            Colonel Whittlesey was selected president.

            May 9. The Cleveland Academy of Medicine was
            established. It merged with The Medical and
            Pathological Society in September, 1873, to

form The Cleveland Medical Association.

May 28. The historical department of the
Cleveland Library Association was created,
adopting the name of Western Reserve Historical Society on June 5.

September. The city bought its first fire
engine of the first class, a rotary power
Silsby.

1868   Dr. Myra K. Herrick led in the organization
of the Homeopathic College for Women, because
the Western Homeopathic College suspended
the granting of medical degrees to women.

The State Legislature granted more control of
the Cleveland Public Schools to the Board of
Education.

January 14. The East Cleveland Railroad Company was granted its routes on Garden Street.

February. The Cleveland Firemen's Relief
Association was formed.

June 17. The Cleveland, Painesville & Ashtabula Railway was changed to the Lake Shore
Railway Company.

July 14. The Independent Order of B'nai Brith
dedicated the Jewish Orphan Asylum.

August 1. The Citizens Saving and Loan
Association was formed, with J. H. Wade as
its first president, and a capital of
$1,000,000. It was authorized by the state
legislature. Associations of this nature
were established to aid people in building
homesteads, and for other purposes.

October 20. The Woman's Christian Association of Cleveland was organized.

1869   Bishop Rappe founded the Home of the Good
Sheperd for wayward girls.

February 17. The Cleveland Public Library
was established by the Board of Education.

March 2. The Peoples Saving and Loan Association was organized with a capital of
$100,000, and D. P. Rhodes as president.

April 5. Mayor Buhner was reelected.

May. A lodge of the Knights of Pythias was organized on the West Side.

May 7. The Legislature passed the enabling act for the creation of Lake View Park.

May 8. The Michigan Southern & North Indiana Railroad was merged with the Lake Shore to form the Lake Shore & Michigan Southern Railroad operating from Erie to Chicago. On August 10, the Buffalo & Erie Railway was absorbed.

July 3. The Main Street Bridge was completed. It was rebuilt in 1885.

October. In a meeting at the Weddell House, educators formed an organization which was the beginning of the Northeastern Ohio Teachers Association.

December 7. The Brooklyn Street Railway Company was given a charter for twenty years.

December 18. The Law Library Association was organized. It adopted its constitution on January 8, 1870.

1870   The population was 92,829.

The Little Sisters of the Poor opened a temporary asylum for the aged poor.

January 10. Standard Oil Company was incorporated under Ohio Laws by John D. Rockefeller, Henry M. Flagler, Samuel Andrews, Stephen V. Harkness and William Rockefeller.

July 2. The Lake Shore & Turcarawas Valley Railroad was incorporated. On November 23, 1893 the road was consolidated with the Cleveland & Southern Railroad, and called the Cleveland, Lorain & Wheeling Railroad.

August. Rt. Rev. Amadeus Rappe resigned as Bishop of the Cleveland Diocese. The Very Rev. Edward Hannone was in charge of the diocese until April, 1872.

August 16. President Ulysses S. Grant passed through the city.

November 1. The United States Weather Bureau office was established in Cleveland.

1871   The Forest City Seminary was opened.

S. H. Laman opened the Empire Hotel.

The office of city auditor was created.

April 3. Frederick W. Pelton was elected Mayor. He served until 1872.

August 22. The City Council created the first board of Park Commissioners. They were granted power to levy a tax for park purposes.

August 31. The Charter for the Valley Railroad was granted. The road was completed in February, 1880.

October 15. The Sunday Morning Voice was established by W. Scott Robison.

1872   The Jefferson Street Bridge was built.

Heinrich Gentz founded the Cleveland Anzeiger. It absorbed the Germania and the Deutsche Presse in 1891. It merged with The Waechter am Erie as the Waechter und Anzeiger.

March 7. The Legislature passed an act establishing a board of Police Commissioners, consisting of the Mayor and four members elected by the people.

Alfred F. Arthur's orchestra gave its first concert in Cleveland.

April 14. Bishop Gilmour was consecrated. He continued in office until his death on April 13, 1891.

July 25. The Cleveland & Mahoning, Liberty & Vienna, and the Niles and New Lisbon Railroads merged as the Cleveland & Mahoning Valley Railway. It was leased to the New York, Pennsylvania & Ohio Railroad Company on July 1, 1880 for eighty-two years.

August. The Protection Company was formed to aid in securing furniture and other valuables taken from the burning buildings.

1872   Fall. The first professional baseball club
             disbanded.

             October 20. The Excelsior Club, a Jewish so-
             cial organization, was founded.

             October 24. The Village of East Cleveland,
             incorporated in 1866, was annexed.

1873   The Park House was built, and served as a
             hotel until 1895.

             Bishop Gilmour helped to establish a shelter
             for children disowned by their parents, and
             the Maternity Home for the Poor.

             February 8. Parts of Brooklyn, Newburgh and
             East Cleveland townships were annexed to
             Cleveland.

             February 17. Henry M. Stanley, who found
             David Livingstone in Central Africa on No-
             vember 10, 1871, delivered his lecture "How
             I Found Dr. Livingstone."

             March 22. The Cleveland Bar Association was
             established at a meeting in the law library
             room.

             April 4. Orlando J. Hodge organized the
             Cleveland Society for the Prevention of
             Cruelty to Animals.

             April 7. Charles A. Otin was elected Mayor.

             April 29. A Board of Fire Commissioners,
             consisting of the Mayor, chairman of the
             Council committee on fire and water, and
             three citizens appointed by the Mayor was es-
             tablished. This committee was eventually
             abolished.

             August 26. The Broadway & Newburgh Street
             Railway received its first grant for twenty
             years.

             October. Harriet Beecher Stowe delivered a
             reading from Uncle Tom's Cabin and the
             Minister's Wooing.

             November 16. The village of Newburgh was
             annexed.

1874   D. Black & Company began a new industry by producing ready-to-wear cloaks for women.

Alfred Arthur established the Cleveland School of Music.

Bishop Gilmour had a colony of Sisters of Notre Dame come from Germany to establish an academy for girls.

January 14. The Union of American Hebrew Congregations, organized in 1873, held its first council in Cleveland.

February 3. The Lake View & Collamer Railroad Company promoted by John D. Rockefeller and others, was chartered.

March 10. The Superior Street Railway Company was chartered.

March 13. The Women's Christian Temperance League was established, with Sarah Fitch as president.

June 16. The South Side Railroad Company was given its original twenty-year grant. Ground was broken on August 16.

July 4. Rev. T. P. Thorpe began editing The Catholic Universe.

July 28. The Woodland Hills Street Railway Company was granted a charter for twenty years.

August. The Euclid Hotel was opened.

September 9. The first lacrosse game was played between the Onondaga Indians and the Victorias of London, Ontario. The Indians won.

1875   The Marine Hospital was leased to a private organization, the Cleveland City Hospital Supply Company.

The Hebrew Relief Association was formed.

The Altenheim Association was organized as a charitable effort to aid the aged.

April 5. Nathan P. Payne was elected Mayor.

September 6. John A. Ellsler opened the new
Euclid Avenue Opera House.

1876   The Women's Christian Association (YWCA) established the Home for Aged Gentlewomen.

The Board of Health was abolished, and its
work given to the Board of Police Commissioners. The Board of Health was restored in
1880, and then the Department of Police was
givem the duties in 1892.

The first art club in Cleveland was begun.

The Cleveland & Berea Street Railway Company
was organized, but never exercised its full
franchise privileges.

January 1. The Ohio National Bank was established with a capital stodk of $600,000, and
Robert Hanna as president.

July 6. Leonard Case gave the library building and Case Hall to the Cleveland Library
Association.

1877   Chief Murphy introduced the patrol and exchange system.

Sunday editions of the _Leader_ and the _Herald_
appeared.

The first aerial ladder was brought to the
city for the use of the fire department.

February 13. The Plain Dealer Publishing
Company was incorporated.

February 24. Leonard Case delivered the
trust deed to Henry G. Abbey, who was to establish The Case School of Applied Science.
The articles of incorporation were filed in
April, 1880.

April. William G. Rose was elected Mayor.

June. The militia in Cleveland organized the
15th Regiment of the Ohio National Guard,
under the National Guard Law.

1878   William Hollinger organized a baseball team.

Dr. Myra K. Merrick led the women doctors in

organizing the Women's and Children's Free
Medical and Surgical Dispensary.

May 14. The first attempt at a comprehensive
Municipal Code in Ohio, rehabilitated the
Mayor as executive, and strengthened the
Council.

November 2. The first issue of The Frankfort
Street Handbill appeared.

1879   The Cleveland baseball team joined the Na-
         tional League, and continued until the 1884
         season, when five of its star players were
         lost to an outlaw league. The club then
         joined the American Association.

         The South Cleveland Banking Company was or-
         ganized with a capital of $150,000, and Jo-
         seph Terney as president.

         R. R. Herrick was elected Mayor and served
         until 1882.

         January 27. The first extensive electric
         illumination in the country was created at
         the Public Square.

         June. The South Cleveland Banking Company
         was organized.

         September 23. A telephone was placed into
         service in a room of the Board of Trade
         Building.

         November 19. The Early Settlers' Associa-
         tion was formed.

1880   The Cleveland Vessel Owners Association was
         established with Captain Alva Bradley as
         its first president.

         The Board of Health was reestablished with a
         group of medical men in charge.

         February 28. The Civil Engineers Club, later
         the Cleveland Engineering Society, was es-
         tablished.

         March 20. The City Armory opened.

         April 6. The Articles of Incorporation of
         The Case School of Applied Science were filed.

September 20. Amassa Stone agreed to give Western Reserve College $500,000 if it moved from Hudson to Cleveland, and its name be changed to Adelbert College of Western Reserve University in memory of his son, who was drowned while a student at Yale.

1881   The Firemen's Pension Fund was begun.

The Sir Moses Montefiore Kester Home for Aged and Infirm Israelites was established. It opened in June, 1882.

The Cleveland Stock Yards Company was incorporated.

The Charity Organization Society was established to reduce pauperism. J. H. Wade was its president.

January 2. B. E. Harris brought the first ambulance to Cleveland.

February 3. The New York, Chicago and St. Louis Railway Company was organized in New York. It was then registered in Indiana to build the mainline from Cleveland to Chicago.

March. A sliding pole was introduced to take the firemen from their sleeping quarters to the engine floor below.

April 19. The Legislature merged the police insurance and health fund into the newly created pension fund.

July 2. President James A. Garfield was shot in Washington. He died September 19.

September 24. The funeral train bearing the slain President Garfield arrived at the Euclid Avenue Station. Public services were conducted on the Square, September 26. He was buried in Lake View Cemetery.

1882   The newest hotel, the Hawley House, opened.

The city purchased the first chemical fire engine.

January 5. Rufus P. Ranney, and a group of lawyers, organized the Cleveland Law College.

March 15. The Day Nursery and Kindergarten Committee was formed.

May. The first steel-workers' strike in Cleveland occurred, when the men in the Newburgh Mills walked off their jobs.

June 23. The Cleveland, Columbus, Cincinnati and Indianapolis Railroad Company purchased the Indianapolis & St. Louis, and St. Louis, Alton & Terre Haute Railroads, and thus opened a through line between Cleveland and St. Louis via Indianapolis.

September 13. J. H. Wade signed a deed giving a gift of land to Cleveland for Wade Park. It was accepted by the Council on September 25.

October. Mrs. S. H. Kimball founded the Cleveland School of Art.

October 6. Mr. E. A. Schellentrager introduced a resolution in the Cleveland Pharmaceutical Society, leading to the establishment of the Cleveland School of Pharmacy.

October 26. Adelbert College of Western Reserve University was dedicated.

November. Cleveland Lodge No. 18 of the Benevolent and Protective Order of Elks was organized.

1883   Street-cleaning machines were introduced.

John Farley was elected Mayor. He served until 1884.

February 13. The State Legislature passed a law giving the city the right to regulate smoke emission.

May 8. The Savings and Trust Company opened with a capital of $75,000. It was the first institution organized under a law permitting trust companies. C. G. King was the first president.

May 21. The Cleveland National Bank was established with a capital of $500,000. S. S. Warner was its first president.

October 22.   The Park Theater opened.   It
burned down January 5, 1884 and was rebuilt.
It reopened September 6, 1886.

1884   When the charter of the Merchants National
            Bank expired, it was reorganized as the
            Mercantile National Bank.

            The Broadway Savings and Trust Company opened
            with $50,000 capital.   Joseph Turney was its
            president.

            The Central Institute opened as a business
            college.   It was incorporated in 1895.

            The Cleveland Training School of Nurses was
            founded by the trustees of the Heron Road
            Hospital.

            The Art Club founded the Cleveland Art
            School.

            March.   The Cleveland Retail Grocers Associa-
            tion was formed.

            March 3.   The Cleveland and Newburgh Rail-
            road Company was incorporated to build a
            railroad from Newburgh to the Cleveland har-
            bor.

            April 11.   The trustees of Western Reserve
            College to establish a university in Cleve-
            land.

            June 7.   The Union National Bank was estab-
            lished with a capital of $1,600,000, under
            George H. Worthington as its first president.

            June 21.   The Cleveland Electric Light Com-
            pany was founded.

            July 26.   The first electric street car in
            America was put into operation in Cleveland.

            December 15.   Charles H. Bulkley, Liberty E.
            Holden and Roman Holden bought the Plain
            Dealer.   They then purchased the Herald in
            1885, so that they could publish morning,
            evening and Sunday editions.

1885   Dr. Frank J. Weed established University Hos-
            pital, which continued until 1894, when its
            place was taken by the Cleveland General

Hospital.

The Cleveland Medical Gazette was revived, and continued until 1902, when it merged into the Cleveland Medical Journal.

George Gardner was elected Mayor.

January. The People's Theater opened.

January 26. The new long-distance telephone was tried out in the office of the Postal Telegraph Company.

February. The Council authorized the Woodland Avenue and West Side Street Railway Companies to merge as The Woodland & West Side Street Railway Company.

February 6. The Cleveland Athletic Club was organized with C. A. Billings as president.

June 7. The Hollenden Hotel was opened.

October 19. The Cleveland Theater opened.

1886   The Women's Christian Association (YWCA) established the Educational and Industrial Union to teach girls sewing, millinary, cooking and stenography.

February 23. Mayor George W. Gardner offered a resolution to the board of commisioners providing for competitive examinations for police force applications. This resolution when passed, established the civil service in the city.

April 30. The State Legislature authorized the Board of Health to appoint sanitary policemen.

May 19. A law was passed establishing a Board of Elections to supervise city and county elections. The Board was organized on June 5.

July. Dr. Cady Staley became the first president of Case School of Applied Science.

August 4. The city's first fireboat was launched.

September 6. St. Ignatius College opened
under the leadership of Father John C. B.
Neustich. The College was the forerunner
of John Carroll University, which was incorporated in 1890.

October 6. The Cleveland Dental Society was
formed with Dr. D. R. Jennings as president.

1887   The German American Savings Bank Company with
a capital of $50,000, and the East End Sa-
vings Bank with a capital of $200,000 were
formed.

February 1. The Cleveland Press Club was
organized.

April 17. The Cleveland Architectural Club
was formed.

July. The Petrie Street Bridge was completed.

July 2. The first number of Church Life, a
publication of the Episcopal Diocese of O-
hio, appeared with W. W. Williams as editor.
It soon became a monthly.

September 12. The Columbia Theater was o-
pened. Its name was changed to the Star
Theater in 1889.

November 3. Dr. D. R. Travis was elected
first surgeon of the fire department.

December. The Society of the Medical Sci-
ences of Cleveland was formed. Its last
meeting was held February 18, 1896.

1888   B. D. Babcock was elected Mayor.

James J. Hill of St. Paul incorporated the
Northern Steamship Company.

The Hebrew Observer, first Jewish newspaper,
appeared.

January. William P. Rose began editing the
Cleveland Town Topics.

January 21. The Young Men's Hebrew Association was organized.

July 23. The statue of Moses Cleaveland,
the city's founder, was unveiled in Public
Square.

September. A college for women was opened.
It was later called Flora Stone Mather College. In March, 1889, Mrs. James F. Clark
gave $100,000 for a building, and the endow-
ment of a professorship.

October. The Eliza Jennings Home for needy
women with incurable ailments was opened by
the Women's Christian Association.

1889   The West Side Citizens League was formed.

The Cleveland Spiders baseball team was admitted to the National League.

The City Hospital was built.

The Permanent Savings and Loan Company was
organized. Its name was changed to the Central Trust Company in 1901.

March 8. John Huntington gave $200,000 worth
of stocks to establish the John Huntington
Benevolent Association, which would in turn
found the John Huntington Polytechnic Institute.

May 4. The Epworth League was formed through
a merger of young people's societies. In
1939 it was renamed the Methodist Youth Fel-
lowship.

August 29. The Cleveland Daily World first
appeared. It was the survivor of the Sunday
World, formerly the Sunday Journal, which
had been published by the Evening Star.

Fall. The Morning Times was published. It
was purchased by Charles A. Otis along with
the afternoon edition of the Plain Dealer
and the News and Herald.

October 11. Three street railway lines on
St. Clair, Superior and Payne Avenues were
merged as the Cleveland Railroad Company.

1890   Homer B. Hatch and Carroll B. Ellinwood formed
a YMCA choir, which became the Singers Club
of Cleveland in 1893.

University School was founded as a college
preparatory institution.

The Cleveland Medical College was formed as
a result of dissension among the faculty of
The Cleveland University of Medicine and
Surgery. The breach was healed in 1897, when
the institution was called The Cleveland
Homeopathic Medical College.

January. Cleveland Lodge No. 4 of the International Ship Masters Association was established. Captain Edward Kelley was first
president of the group.

March 17. George J. Bailey, and a few
friends, all of whom wete tax collectors, began the development of a chapter of the American Philatelic Association. Later the name
was changed to the Garfield-Perry Stamp Club.

May 26. The Central National Bank opened
with a capital of $800,000. Its first presi-
dent was George H. Ely.

May 29. The Garfield Monument in memory of
President James A. Garfield was dedicated.

June 16. Reservoir Park was created out of
the old Kentucky Street Reservoir. Its name
was changed to Fair View in 1897.

July 13-15. The Central Conference of American Rabbis, founded by Dr. Isaac M. Wise of
Cincinnati, held its first regular meeting
in Cleveland.

August 5. The management of the Cleveland
baseball team purchased Denton T. "Cy" Young
from the Canton, Ohio Club for $200.

November 10. Part of Brooklyn Village was
annexed.

December 4. Horace Kelley died. He left his
real estate to be used to found an art gal-
lery and school.

1891   The Lake Erie Yacht Racing Association was
organized.

The Cleveland Athletic Basebal Club played
its first season.

The Cleveland Belt & Terminal Railroad was incorporated to speed the movement of freight.

St. Clair Hospital was organized.

William G. Rose was elected Mayor.

May 1. League Park, the home of Cleveland's major league club, opened.

September 12. The Szabadsag a Hungarian paper, meaning "Liberty," was first published.

October. The Dental Department of the Cleveland University of Medicine and Surgery opened.

November 10. Andrew Squire led in the formation of the Park and Boulevard Association to urge creation of a park and boulevard system.

December 19. The Western Reserve Chapter of the Daughters of the American Revolution was organized with Mrs. Elroy M. Avery as the first president.

1892   The Tavern Club for socialites and sportsmen was formed.

The Cleveland and Buffalo Transit Company was organized.

St. John's Hospital was established as an offshoot of St. Alexis Hospital by Bishop Gilmour.

The Garfield Savings Bank Company was organized with H. Clark Ford as president.

The Wick Banking and Trust Company was created from the private bank of Henry Wick & Company. In 1901, The City Trust Company took over its business.

February. The Rowfant Club was organized for book lovers and collectors with John C. Covert as president.

March. Right Rev. Ignatius F. Horstmann was appointed Bishop of Cleveland. Bishop Gilmour had died in 1891.

The Dental School of Western Reserve University was established.

March 7. The Western Reserve Historical Society was incorporated.

March 8. The State Legislature adopted Colonel John M. Wilcox's proposal for a federal plan of municipal government, which continued until the Supreme Court declared it to be unconstitutional in 1904.

March 12. The first branch of the Cleveland Public Library System opened on Pearl Street as the West Side Branch.

April. William G. Rose was reelected Mayor.

April 28. The Lake Carriers Association was formed to press for improvements in Lake Erie.

May 5. The Western Reserve Society of the Sons of the American Revolution was chartered. Elroy M. Avery was the first president.

June 21. The Cleveland Real Estate Board with Daniel R. Taylor as first president was established to stop unscrupulous competition in the real estate business.

July. The Western Reserve National Bank with a capital of $1,000,000 was opened. James Pickards was the first president. It was absorbed by the Bank of Commerce, N.A. in 1899.

September 28. A portion of East Cleveland Township was annexed.

1893   The Cleveland Day School for deaf children opened.

The first police matrons were introduced.

The German Hospital for the German population was opened.

February 3. The Cleveland Medical Society was formed with Dr. W. J. Scott as president.

February 6. The Board of Trade was reorganized under the new name of The Cleveland
Chamber of Commerce.

April. Robert Blee was elected Mayor.

The City Council approved a franchise for
long distance telephone service. The Midland Company was the first firm in the field.

May 15. An ordinance permitted creation of
the Cleveland City Railway Company and consolidation of the Superior, St. Clair and
Woodland Avenue and West Side Lines.

May 29. The Cleveland Electric Railway Company was authorized, unifying the Broadway,
Newburg, East Cleveland and South Side Companies.

July 22. A committee was appointed by the
Early Settlers Association to meet with the
City Council, Chamber of Commerce and other
groups to plan for Cleveland's centennial,
July 22, 1896.

October 2. The Waechter am Erie and the
Cleveland Anzeiger merged to form the
Waechter und Anzeiger.

The first issue of the Evening Post, a penny
paper, appeared. It was formerly the Evening
Plain Dealer.

October 23. Gordon Park was given to the
city from the estate of William J. Gordon.

November 21. The Chamber of Commerce appointed a committee to plan for the celebration of the city's centennial.

1894   Robert E. McKisson was elected Mayor.

The Law and Order Association of Cleveland
was founded.

Edgewater Park was acquired with a frontage
of 6,000 feet on the Lake.

A Personal Service Society was established,
and then merged with the newly formed Council
of Jewish Women. The latter was established
by consolidation of The Ladies' Benevolent

Society and The Ladies' Sewing Society.

St. John's Hospital, run by the Franciscan Sisters, was opened.

The Village of West Cleveland was annexed.

The West Cleveland Banking Company was organized with a capital of $100,000. W. J. White was president.

April 30. Brooklyn Village joined with Cleveland.

June 28. The Guardian Trust Company was incorporated with a capital of $500,000, which was doubled by October 1.

July 4. The Soldiers and Sailors Monument was dedicated.

September 10. The Cleveland Trust Company with a capital of $500,000 was organized, with J. G. W. Cowles as president.

October. The Cleveland & Elyria Electric Railway Company was chartered. It opened December, 1895. On December 2, 1897, a consolidation led to the formation of the Cleveland, Berea, Elyria & Oberlin Railway Company. A further merge occurred in December, 1902.

November. The Akron, Bedford & Cleveland Railway Company was chartered.

The Temple Society was established by Tifereth Israel Congregation, which conducted University Extension Classes and Popular Lectures.

November 7. The Cleveland Medical Library Association was organized with Dr. Joseph E. Cook as president.

November 17. The Women's Christian Temperance Union held its national convention in Cleveland, its birthplace.

November 20. The first meeting of the Cleveland Council of Jewish Women was held.

December 10. The Guardian Trust Company opened with $500,000 capital.

1895   The Cleveland & Southwestern Traction Com-
          pany was organized.

          Henry P. McIntosh presided over the organi-
          zation of the Colonial Club.

          A boys' club, girls' sewing school and wo-
          man's guild were formed in the basement of
          the Old Stone Church. This was the nucleus
          of the Goodrich Settlement established in
          1897.

          The Shaker Heights Land Company donated
          278.85 acres to the city for Shaker Heights
          Park.

          St. Mary's Home for Young Women was opened.

          January. A Woman's edition of the Plain
          Dealer was issued with Mrs. Howard M. Ingra-
          ham as editor-in-chief.

          March 19. Marcus A. Hanna announced the
          Presidential candidacy of William McKinley
          at the Forest City House.

          April 15. The Cleveland, Painesville & East-
          ern Railway Company was incorporated. It o-
          pened July 4, 1896.

          May. Mayor Robert E. McKisson and Wilson M.
          Day, president of the Cleveland Chamber of
          Commerce, along with others, appointed a
          commission to direct the city's Centennial
          Celebration in 1896.

          May 31. The Press Club was formed.

          June 4. Ground was broken for the new City
          Hall.

          June 14. The Cleveland Orchestra was formed.

          September 9. The Cleveland Recorder first
          appeared.

          Fall. Cleveland won first place in the Na-
          tional League pennant race, defeating the
          Baltimore Orioles.

          December. The Cleveland & Elyria Electric
          Railway opened a 17-mile road.

1896   The Cleveland Society of the Archaeological
        Institute of America was formed.

        Drs. P. Maxwell Foshay and Henry S. Upson
        began editing The Cleveland Journal of Medi-
        cine. It merged after five years with the
        Cleveland Medical Gazette into The Cleveland
        Medical Journal.

        Miss Jennie Warren Prentiss opened a private
        school for girls. It grew into the Wade
        Park Home for Girls, and was incorporated
        as the Laurel Institute in 1899.

        The Froebel School was established by parents
        for individualized instruction.

        Commissioners bought the Dunham, Rittberger
        and Carter farms for $32,229.64, and created
        Newburgh Park.

        The Cleveland Savings and Banking Company
        opened with William M. Day as president.

        Free kindergartens were opened in Cleveland.

        January. The Euclid Avenue Savings and Bank-
        ing Company began business, when it absorbed
        the Arcade Savings Bank Company.

        May. The Lutheran Hospital was organized.

        July 4. The Cleveland, Painesville & Eastern
        Railway opened.

        CLEVELAND AT ONE HUNDRED

        July 19. Cleveland's One Hundredth Anniver-
        sary celebration officially opened.

        July 22. J. G. W. Cowles, president of the
        Chamber of Commerce announced that John D.
        Rockefeller was giving 276 acres along Doan
        Brook to the city for a park, along with
        $300,000 to pay for improvements made in
        that area.

        August 22-29. Eight thousand members of the
        Knights of Pythias camped in Cleveland in a
        city of tents.

        September 1. The Cleveland Home for Aged

People was incorporated.

1897   The Department of Forestry and Fisheries was established.

The Cleveland Law School was incorporated.

The American Exchange National Bank was organized.

February 22. The South Side Branch Library building was opened.

May 18. The Dow Chemical Company was incorporated.

Summer. Judge Bentley, Mr. Rowley and Judge Willis Vickery worked with Baldwin University at Berea, Ohio, to establish Baldwin University Law School.

William G. Webster of Chicago, Sherman Arter, Judge F. J. Wing, Judge Neff, and others began the Cleveland Law School.

In the Summer of 1899 the two abovementioned schools merged under the name of the Cleveland Law School of Baldwin University.

July 9. The city was equipped with new street signs.

October 6. The Lorain & Cleveland Railway was opened from Rocky River to Lorain.

1898   The Gatling gun, a rapid-fire weapon developed in Cleveland by Richard Jordan Gatling, was going to revolutionize gun-making.

Frank Dettaus Robison transferred the Cleveland National League baseball club to St. Louis.

The western portion of Glenville was added to the city.

January 15. The College Club was established to promote social, philanthropic and literary interests.

February 6. The Knights of Columbus granted the first Cleveland Charter to Gilmour Council.

April 17. The Lake Shore Line from Willoughby to Cleveland was put into operation.

June 8. The University Club of Cleveland
was incorporated.

November. The Cleveland Retail Credit Men's
Company was organized.

1899   David May and associates purchased E. R. Hall
& Dutton Company to found The May Company of
Cleveland, which was destined to become the
May Stores.

The Brotherhood of Railroad Trainmen, organized September 23, 1883, moved to Cleveland
from Peoria, Illinois.

The State Legislature passed a law providing
for the regulation of the civil service in
the police department.

Washington Park was created.

John Farley was elected Mayor. He served
until 1900.

March. The Cleveland Stock Exchange opened
with a membership fee of $100. James Par-
malee was elected president.

April. The Educational Alliance Council of
Jewish groups was formed.

April 19. Businessmen met to form a Convention League to bring conventions to Cleveland.

May. The State Banking and Trust Company
was formed with $300,000 capital.

August 10. The Health Department ruled that
all manufacturing plants must be provided
with smoke consumers.

1900   The population was 361,768.

The Hebrew Observer merged with the Jewish
Review to form The Jewish Review and Observer.

The city acquired Woodland Hills Park.

Davis P. Hawley and M. E. Gaul formed the
Cleveland Bluebirds baseball club with John
Kilfoyle as president. They joined the re-
organized Western League, and later the
American League.

The Jewish Women's Hospital Society was
formed.

January 8. The Cleveland Automobile Club
was organized.

May. The Bethel Associated Charities was
incorporated.

June 8. The Retail Merchants Board was
formed as a division of the Chamber of Commerce.

October 15. William Jennings Bryan closed
his Presidential tour of Ohio with a speech
in Cleveland.

1901   W. J. White built the New Amsterdam Hotel.

The Cleveland, Painesville & Ashtabula Railway Company was chartered. It opened September 21, 1903.

The Empire Theater opened.

May. Tom L. Johnson bacame Mayor. He served
for eight years until 1909.

September 25. The Lakeshore Railway received
its charter.

November 27. The Cleveland Advertising Club
was formed.

1902   The Visiting Nurse Association came into
existence.

Spring elections were abolished. Municipal
and county elections were to take place on
the first Tuesday after the first Monday in
November.

The State Legislature established a uniform
municipal code for all cities and towns in
Ohio.

A portion of Glenville Village was annexed

to Cleveland.

April. The Cleveland Congress of Mothers was organized at the Old Stone Church.

May. The Legislature created the Juvenile Court, attached to the Court of Insolvency.

May 9. The by-laws and constitution of the Cleveland Federation of Women's Clubs were adopted.

May 28. The Cuyahoga County Medical Society merged with the Cleveland Medical Society to form the Academy of Medicine of Cleveland.

June. The Supreme Court ruled against the structures and classification of cities in Ohio in various cases.

1903 A Winton runabout, built in Cleveland, was the first motor car to cross the United States.

The Public Library organized a library for the blind.

An independent Department of Health was established. It was abolished in 1907.

New central telegraph equipment was purchased for the fire department at a cost of $25,500.

The Prospect Theater opened.

January 17. The Cleveland Trust Company system of branch banking was inaugurated.

February 9. The city began to receive natural gas.

March 16. The Colonial Theater opened.

November 17. The Federation of Jewish Charities was chartered.

1904 John D. Rockefeller donated $200,000 for the establishment of physics and mining engineering laboratories at Case Institute.

The Reserve Trust Company was organized with Luther Allen as president. It was placed in the hands of a receiver in 1908.

Western Reserve University established its school of library science with a gift from Andrew Carnegie.

February 15. Marcus Alonzo Hanna died. President Theodore Roosevelt, members of his cabinet, and other leading figures paid their respects in Cleveland.

April 11. The village of Linndale was annexed to Cleveland.

July 18. The first Carnegie branch of the Public Library, the Woodland Public Library, opened.

November. Orlando G. and Fernando Melaragno established the Voco del Popolo Italiano, an Italian newspaper.

1905   The Anti-Tuberculosis League, with the aid of the Associated Charities and the Visiting Nurse Association, convinced the city to care for and control tuberculosis by employing nurses.

The News was first published.

The Legal Aid Society was organized and incorporated.

The Gemilath Chesed Society was formed. It was reorganized in 1907 as the Hebrew Free Loan Association.

The Superior Savings and Trust Company was formed with a capital of $500,000. J. J. Sullivan was president.

April. Construction of the Belt Line Railroad began.

April 14-15. The St. Clair Branch Library was opened to the public.

May. The first S. S. Kresge store in Cleveland opened on the site of the future May Company.

June 19. The village of Glenville became part of Cleveland.

September 15. The village of Corlett and

part of Newburgh Heights was annexed.

December. The first issue of The Dentists Magazine, a monthly appeared. In 1909, it was made a part of the Dental Summary.

December 11. The village of South Brooklyn, incorporated in 1889, was annexed.

1906   The Orthodox Old Home for aged and friendless Jewish men and women opened.

The Baptist Home of Northern Ohio was organized.

St. Anthony's Home for boys opened.

The St. Luke's Hospital Association was formed. It was succeeded by Cleveland General Hospital in 1934.

January 15. The Broadway Branch Library was opened.

March 9. The Jewish Independent first appeared.

March 23. The Miles Park Library Branch building was opened.

August 23. Mayor Johnson proposed formation of a holding company by the Cleveland Electric Railway Company, including the Forest City Railway. He also favored a three-cent fare and penny transfer. There was a great deal of opposition.

November 1. The three-cent streetcar fare was put into effect on the line from Denison Avenue to Detroit Avenue.

December. The Infants Clinic Hospital of Cleveland was incorporated. It became the Babies Dispensary and Hospital on February 6, 1907.

1907   Dr. C. Lee Graber, and several other physicians incorporated Lakewood Hospital.

City officials voted to move the zoo from Wade to Brookside Park.

The Depositors Savings and Trust Company was
organized with $300,000 capital. Tom L.
Johnson was its president. Its accounts
were taken over in 1909 by the First National
Bank and The Cleveland Trust Company.

January 23. The Hough Avenue Branch Library
building was opened.

January 25. The Cleveland Chamber of Industry was incorporated to foster the interests
of the West Side. It merged with the Chamber
of Commerce in October, 1930.

March 4. Several interurban street railway
lines were merged into the Cleveland, Southwestern & Columbus Railway.

Summer. The Council of Jewish Women, and the
Council of Educational Alliance opened Camp
Wise for boys and girls. Dr. Samuel D. Wise
offered free use of his property along the
east shore of Lake Erie.

August 27. The Cleveland Life Insurance Company was organized with William H. Hunt as
president.

September 30. The Standard Club, a Jewish
social group, was organized.

Fall. The Cleveland Dental Library was begun as a result of Dr. Charles R. Strong's
desire to donate his dental library.

November. Rev. Wilson R. Stearly organized
the West End Neighborhood House to aid
immigrants.

December. The Hippodrome opened.

1908   The Americke Delnicke Listy, a Bohemian
            weekly, was established.

The second Cleveland Athletic Club was organized.

St. Luke's Hospital opened.

April 27. Mayor Johnson and his friends were
victorious in fostering the sale of the
franchises and property of the Forest City
Railway Company, the Municipal Traction Com-

pany, the Low Fare Railway Company, and the
Neutral Street Railway to The Cleveland
Railway Company.

April 29. The State Legislature passed the
Paine Law, modifying the form of municipal
government, with the mayor as the chief
executive officer of the city, elected for
a two-year term.

May 1. The Jewish Daily Press, a Yiddish
paper, was first published.

May 16. The Jewish Religious Education
Association of Ohio was formed with Rabbi
Grier as president.

June 29. The National Education Association
met in Cleveland.

October 23. The citizens of Cleveland voted
in a referendum to return the streetcar system to private ownership.

1909   The advertising clubs of Cleveland, Detroit
and Buffalo organized the Advertising Affilia-
tion.

May 13. Bishop Horstmann died. Monsignor
F. M. Boff was given temporary charge of the
diocese until June 16.

June 19. Right Rev. John Patrick Farrelly,
D.D., was installed as the fourth Bishop of
Cleveland.

July 1. The Hiram House was opened for social
settlement work.

December 18. The Taylor Grant traction plan
became law, with a sliding-fare scale for
the trolleys, and limiting profits to six
percent, with the city council in control of
street railway operations.

1910   The first Boy Scout troops were formed in
Cleveland at the West Side Branch of the
YMCA.

The Cleveland College of Physicians and
Surgeons merged with the School of Medicine
of Western Reserve University.

The Sunbeam School for Crippled Children opened.

Taxicabs were introduced into Cleveland.

A branch of the National Association of Colored People was established.

The Rocky River and Harvand-Denison Bridges were completed.

January 7. The South Cleveland Banking Company was forced to close because of large loans to the Werner Publishing Company.

January 21. Collinwood was annexed.

November. Herman C. Buehr was elected Mayor and served until 1911.

1911   January 16. Sylvia Pankhurst, English suffragist, and Emma Goldman, anarchist, visited Cleveland.

June 5. The Legislature passed an act, inspired by Cleveland groups, authorizing establishment of parks, boulevards and public grounds outside the city limits for recreation.

June 21. Cleveland was the third American city to establish a department of neurology in the public schools.

August. The Phyllis Wheatley Association was established to provide a home for Negro girls.

September 23. Mrs. Rose Constant became the first female police officer in the city, when she became a sanitary inspector.

November. Newton D. Baker was elected Mayor, serving until 1915.

1912   When Newton D. Baker took office, he indicated he would work for home rule, and eventually was able to have a new charter passed.

A Municipal Court was established.

April 7. The City Council approved a lot-

garden plan. Citizens took up lot-gardening
to reduce the cost of living and beautify
the city.

June. The YWCA West Side Branch opened.

August 1. The Women's Art Club was organized.

September 3. Cleveland voters chose to assume
all local self-government powers, and elected
fifteen commissioners to frame a home-rule
charter for the city.

September 6. The Junior League was formed
with Mrs. John Cross as president.

October 12. The City Club of Cleveland was
incorporated.

October 19. The Hotel Statler opened.

1913   George Adomeit and Charles Shackleton formed
            the Cleveland Society of Artists.

The Jewish Hospital Association of Cleveland opened the East Side Free Dispensary.

Samuel Rocker established the weekly <u>Jewish
World</u>. It then became a daily, and later
a weekly again.

March 2. Max Faetkenheuer opened the Metropolitan Theater.

May 1. The Cleveland Federation for Charity
and Philanthropy was organized. It budgeted
available funds for the Cleveland Welfare
agencies.

June 20. The Cleveland Association of
Building Owners and Managers was incorporated.

1914   The Mall Theater was constructed.

March 3. An ordinance went into effect re-
quiring all vehicles to have tail lights.

May 3. The Tom L. Johnson Monument was unveiled in Library Park.

May 14. The grade school teachers formed a
union. They won their fight with the Board
of Education to maintain the union on June 9.

November 16. The Federal Reserve Bank of
Cleveland was opened.

1915   The East Cleveland Hospital was organized.

The Musical Arts Association was formed.
David Z. Norton was its first president.

The Lithuanian weekly newspaper, Dirva,
first appeared.

May 12-14. The World Court Congress met in
Cleveland. Former President William Howard
Taft attended.

June 6. The City of Buffalo was the first
ship to land at the new lake terminal.

June 15. Mayor Newton D. Baker appointed
the first City Plan Commission.

November 2. Harry L. Davis was elected
Mayor. He served from 1916 to 1920. The
preferential system of voting was put into
effect for mayoral candidates.

1916   The Cleveland Greys became F Company of the
Ohio National Guard. It served with General
John J. Pershing against Pancho Villa in
Mexico. The latter had raided a border town
in New Mexico.

The City Council passed an ordinance re-
quiring pasteurization of milk.

The Cleveland Hospital Council was organized
to promote efficiency and cooperation between
various hospitals. It was incorporated in
1918.

The Stillman Theater, a motion picture house,
was opened.

A committee was appointed to study proposals
for the city manager plan of government for
the city.

January 18. The Women's City Club was organized. The Downtown Club merged with it.

March 8. The Morris Plan Bank of Cleveland
was organized. It became the Bank of Ohio
Company in 1946.

March 10.   Former Mayor Newton D. Baker was
appointed Secretary of War by President
Woodrow Wilson.

May 18.   The first Kiwanis national convention was held in Cleveland.

June 6.   The Cleveland Museum of Art opened
in Wade Park.

·July 4.   The new City Hall was dedicated.

August 11-13.   A milk strike occurred in the
city.

September.   Western Reserve University organized the School of Applied Social Science.

1917   The Cleveland Heights Women's Club was
formed.

The Americanization Board was established
to help draft officials in their work with
foreign born residents.

The Cleveland Federation for Charity and
Philanthropy, and the Welfare Council united
to form the Welfare Federation of Cleveland,
with Martin A. Marks president.

April.   The Brotherhood of Locomotive Firemen and Engineers established its headquar-
ters in Cleveland.

April 4.   Mayor Harry L. Davis appointed an
Advisory War Board to plan war activities
for the city.

May 6.   Lakeside Unit, Base Hospital No. 4,
left for the Atlantic coast.   It was Cleveland's first official contribution to the
United States forces.

June 15.   Theresa Steerer was the first woman
admitted to Western Reserve University Law
School.

July 6.   The Lakeside Hospital received
$1,000,000 under the will of Colonel O. H.
Payne.

August 30.   The Cleveland Plain Dealer purchased The Morning Leader.

September 1. The Lake Division of the American Red Cross was founded.

December 17. The Negro Welfare Association was established.

1918   June 14. The afternoon papers raised their prices.

December 16. The Cleveland Hotel was opened.

1919   The Cleveland Safety Council was organized.

The Catholic Charities Corporation was organized.

January 1. When the firemen went on an eight-hour day in defiance of the authorities, Mayor Davis asked former servicemen to take their place.

January 10. The Board of Education decided to continue military training in the high schools, in order to promote physical fitness.

July 5. Motormen and conductors of the Cleveland Street Railway Company went out on strike. It ended July 7.

October. Two reports were issued by the Committee investigating the City Manager Plan. A majority urged adoption of the manager form of government, and a minority favored retention of the existing administration.

November. William S. Fitzgerald was elected Mayor. He served from 1920 to 1921.

1920   The population was 796,841.

The Cleveland Chapter of the Veterans of Foreign Wars was organized.

The Cleveland Recreation Council was organized.

April 22. The League of Women Voters was created.

May 21. Mayor Fitzgerald ordered that all gambling houses be closed.

October. The Cleveland Lions Club was
chartered.

November. Fred Kohler was elected Mayor.
He served from 1921 to 1923.

November 14. The six-cent street car fare
went into effect, with one-cent for transfers.

December 5. The Deaconess Evangelical Hospital was established.

December 13. The Cleveland Museum of Natural
History was chartered.

1921   The Children's Bureau was organized.

The Flora Stone Mather College for women of
Western Reserve University established a
nursing education department.

March 10. The Board of Education agreed to
permit boxing in the schools.

April. The Midland Bank opened with D. D.
Kimmel as president.

June 5. The Convention of the Zionist Organization of America opened. Albert Ein-
stein was one of the speakers.

September 20. The Ohio State and Ohio Bell
Telephone Companies merged.

1922   A. E. Stouffer initiated the organization
of Stouffer Restaurants.

Radio Station WHK was opened as the first in
Ohio.

March 2. The Commercial, a morning paper,
was first published.

April 15. The Public Auditorium first
opened.

CLEVELAND UNDER THE CITY MANAGER
FORM OF GOVERNMENT

The City Manager from of government was in-
stituted in Cleveland.

May. St. Ignatius College became Cleveland University.

December 6. William Rowland Hopkins was appointed City Manager. Under this new form of government, the City Council President was to serve as Mayor.

1924   January 1. William Rowland Hopkins became the first City Manager. Clayton C. Townes, Council President, served as Mayor until 1925.

April 28. The Metropolitan Opera first came to Cleveland.

June 10-13. The Republican National Convention was held in Cleveland. President Calvin Coolidge was renominated, and General Charles G. Dawes was nominated for Vice President.

1925   The Babies and Children's Hospital opened.

Cleveland College was established. Although it was independent, it was closely affiliated with Western Reserve University.

The Police Women's Bureau was opened.

June 14. The Rotarian International Convention met in the city.

July 1. The Cleveland Municipal Airport opened.

September 15. John D. Marshall became City Council President and Mayor, after Clayton C. Townes resigned. Marshall served until November 7, 1931.

1926   February 23. Billy Sunday, the evangelist, spoke in Cleveland.

May. The Cleveland Chamber of Commerce's official monthly journal, The Clevelander, began publication.

November 10. The Hotel Allerton opened.

1927   January 1. WJAY began broadcasting.

March 3. The Times ceased publishing.

November 17. Various groups urged Mayor
Marshall to establish a committee to study
plans for cooperation of the city and sub-
urbs in a larger governmental unit.

1928   Stout Air Lines began air service between
            Cleveland and Detroit.

            April 28. An amendment to abolish the City
            Manager form of Government was defeated.

1929   The Cleveland Child Health Association was
            established.

            Lake Shore Hospital opened.

            March 13. The first Plain Dealer Golden
            Gloves Boxing Tournament opened.

            August. Cleveland citizens voted to retain
            the City Manager plan.

            December. The Yellow Cab Company of Cleve-
            land was established.

1930   The population was 900,429.

            The Motor Transit Management Company, which
            had come to Cleveland in the 1920's, took
            the name of The Greyhound Management Company.

            January 13. The City Council removed City
            Manager William R. Hopkins from office.

            June 4. Zone fares were introduced on the
            streetcars.

            December 15. WGAR radio station opened in
            the Hotel Statler. In 1937 it joined the
            Columbia Broadcasting System.

1931   August 4-9. The Twentieth Conference of
            the World's Alliance of the Young Men's
            Christian Association met in Cleveland.

            September 7. The Cleveland Symphony Orches-
            tra's new home, Severance Hall, was dedica-
            ted.

            November 3. Cleveland voters decided to dis-
            card the City Manager form of government and
            to return to the system of an elected Mayor
            and ward councilmen.

November 9. Harold H. Burton began serving as Acting Mayor until February 20, 1932.

CLEVELAND: MAYOR AND COUNCIL
FORM OF GOVERNMENT

1932   Miles Heights Village was annexed to Cleveland.

February 16. Ray T. Miller was elected Mayor. He served from February 20, 1932 to November 14, 1933.

September 8. The Rt. Rev. James A. McFadden became Bishop of the Diocese.

1933   January 7. The Plain Dealer bought the Sunday News, and became the city's only morning and Sunday paper.

November 7. Harry L. Davis was elected Mayor defeating the incumbent Ray T. Miller. Davis served from November 14 until November 11, 1935.

1934   The Sight Saving Council of Cleveland was established.

The Sherwin-Williams Company established the Metropolitan Auditions of the Air radio program, as a means of encouraging young talented singers.

1935   Construction was begun on three Public Works Administration slum areas; Cedar-Central Apartments, Outhwaite Homes and Lakeview Terrace.

The Women's Federal Savings & Loan Association was chartered. It was the first to be managed and staffed by women.

April 7. Mayor Davis cut city services because of serious financial difficulties.

October. The Cleveland Osteopathic Hospital and Clinic was formed.

November 5. Harold H. Burton was elected Mayor. He had defeated Mayor Davis in the primary election. Burton served from November 11, 1935 to December 31, 1940.

February 3. The Cleveland College of Western Reserve University offered a form of
cooperative education for men and women
taking business administration courses.

June 11-13. The Republican National Convention met in Cleveland and nominated
Alfred M. Landon of Kansas for President
and Colonel Frank Knox for Vice President.

June 28. The Great Lakes Exposition opened.
President Franklin D. Roosevelt visited it
on August 24. It closed October 8.

September. The American Legion held its national convention in Cleveland.

October 30. The United Broadcasting Company
bought radio station WJAY, and merged it with
WHK. It became WCLE in 1937, when it began
to broadcast Mutual Broadcasting System pro-
grams. It moved to Akron in 1945.

1937   Fenn College bought a 21-story skyscraper at
Euclid and 24th Street as its main campus.

May 23. John D. Rockefeller died at his
estate in Ormond Beach, Florida. His family
had moved to Cleveland in 1853.

May 29. The Great Lakes Exposition opened
for its second season.

September 17. Fort Huntington Park was dedicated.

November. Harold H. Burton was reelected
Mayor.

1938   Jerry Siegel and Joel Shuster sold the first
"Superman" story.

January 9. The Wings Over Jordan, a group
of black singers, made their first appear-
ance over a national program of the Columbia
Broadcasting System on WGAR. This group had
originated as the choir in Gethsemane Baptist Church in 1935.

March 19. The Cleveland Barons won the Wes-
tern Division Championship of the American
Hockey League. They were defeated for the
League Championship by the Providence Reds

on April 12.

March 30. The Cleveland Board of Education
was given permission to proceed with the
opening of WBOE-FM as an educational station.

May 16. The Union Bank of Commerce developed
the Cleveland Plan to advocate the business
of the city.

1939   The Junior Association of Commerce opened.

March 25. Bishop Joseph Schrembs was made
Archbishop.

April 8. The Cleveland Barons won the American Hockey League Championship and the Cal-
der Trophy.

June. Rotary International held its convention in Cleveland.

June 27. The Indians played the first night
game at the Stadium defeating the Detroit
Tigers 5-0. Bob Feller pitched a one-hit
game.

July 4. The first Festival of Freedom was
held at the Stadium.

July 30. A mass dedication was held for the
chain of Cleveland Cultural Gardens, representing various nations and nationalities of
the world, in Rockefeller Park.

September 16. The first American Congress
on Obstetrics and Gynecology met at the
Public Auditorium.

October 6. The Main Avenue Bridge was opened.

November 7. Mayor Burton was reelected for
a third term.

1940   The population was 878,336.

The Cleveland Bar Association received the
1940 award of merit for outstanding public
service by the American Bar Association.

April 1. The Junior Association of Commerce
was welcomed by the Cleveland Chamber of
Commerce.

April 16. Bob Feller pitched the first o-
pening-day no-hit game in modern-league
history.

May 15. The city government announced that
the voters had approved a $4.5 million bond
issue for major highways.

October. The administration of the Cleveland Zoo was entrusted to the Cleveland
Museum of Natural History.

November 17. Mayor Burton announced his resignation because he was elected United
States Senator. Edward Blythin, Director of
Law, was appointed to serve the unexpired
term of Mayor Burton.

December 3. Cleveland was selected as the
site of the Government's new eight million
four hundred thousand dollar engine research
laboratory by the National Advisory Committee
for Aeronautics.

December 3. Edward Blythin became Mayor and
served until November 10, 1941.

1941   April 10. The Barons won the American Hockey
League Western Championship, as well as the
American Hockey League Championship.

Fall. Mrs. Robert H. Jamison and Mrs. Neal
G. Gray launched the local USO unit.

November 4. Frank J. Lausche was elected
Mayor. He assumed office November 10 and
continued until December 31, 1944.

December 1. The wartime plant of the Thompson
Aircraft Products opened.

1942   January 7. The Plain Dealer celebrated its
one hundredth anniversary.

Spring. Mayor Frank J. Lausche formed an
advisory committee to reorganize the City
Plan Commission and make it more effective.

April 23. The Cleveland Street Railway Company was taken over by the city.

May 7. Newspaper prices rose to four cents.

May 28. The *Plain Dealer* aided in the creation of The Blue Star Mothers Service, Inc.

June 25. Mayor Lausche presented Secretary of the Treasury Henry Morgenthau with the bomber fund raised by the people of Cleveland.

August 21. The War Service Center was dedicated.

1943   The Foreign Affairs Council, organized in 1923, was incorporated as the Council on World Affairs.

January 14. The Stage Door Canteen opened.

June 8. The City Council passed an ordinance providing for penalties against black marketeers.

November 2. Frank J. Lausche was reelected Mayor.

November 17. The Most Rev. Edward Francis Hoban was named Coadjutor to Archbishop Joseph Schrembs.

1944   The Barons won the western championship of the American Hockey League.

Mayor Lausche appointed a Post War Planning Council.

January 29. A committee of engineers presented a plan for construction of a freeway.

April 27. The Great Lakes Historical Society was organized.

November. Thomas A. Burke was elected Mayor. He assumed office January 1, 1945 and continued until November, 1953.

1945   April 10. The Barons won the American Hockey League Championship.

November 2. Archbishop Joseph Schrembs died. Bishop Edward F. Hoban became his successor.

November 6. Thomas A. Burke was reelected Mayor.

November 14. The Associated Charities

changed its name to the Family Service Association.

December 16. The Cleveland Rams won the professional football championship, defeating the Washington Redskins 15-14. The Rams' franchise was moved to Los Angeles in January, 1946. The Cleveland Browns became the new football team.

POST WORLD WAR II: URBAN REDEVELOPMENT

1946   The Cleveland World Trade Organization was established to promote knowledge of export and import business.

January 6. The Parking Advisory Committee submitted a comprehensive plan for parking in the city central district to the City Planning Commission.

April 30. Msgr. John R. Hagan was designated as auxiliary to Archbishop Hoban.

June 20. Civil Service employees ended their strike.

September 6. The Cleveland Browns played their first football game in the Stadium against the Miami Seahawks and defeated them 14-0.

November 6. Thomas J. Herbert, born in Cleveland in 1894, was elected governor of Ohio.

December 22. The Cleveland Browns defeated the New York Yankees 14-9 and won the national football championship.

1947   July 1. The Case School of Applied Science became the Case Institute of Technology.

November 4. Mayor Thomas A. Burke was re-elected.

1948   April 11. The Barons won the American Hockey League Championship.

April 20. The Cleveland Chamber of Commerce celebrated its contennial.

October 4. The Indians won the American
League Pennant, defeating the Boston Red
Sox.

October 11. The Cleveland Indians won the
World Series, defeating the Boston Braves
four games to two.

November 29. The Cleveland Browns won the
western division championship of the All-
America Conference.

December 19. The Browns defeated the Buffalo
Bills for the All-America Conference Championship.

1949   November 8. Mayor Burke was reelected.

December 11. The Cleveland Browns defeated
San Francisco 21-7 to win the All-America
Conference Championship.

1950   The population was 914,808.

May 8. The Convention and Visitors Bureau
began a test with 10,000 silver dollars to
show how convention money circulates and aids
prosperity.

December 17. The Cleveland Browns won the
American Division Championship of the National Football League.

December 24. The Cleveland Browns won the
League Championship.

1951   November 6. Mayor Burke was reelected.

December 23. The Los Angeles Rams defeated
the Cleveland Browns, American Division
Champions, for the League Championship.

1952   June 28. The Plain Dealer raised its Sunday
edition price to twenty cents.

July 2. The Cleveland Barons were denied
the right to enter the National Hockey
League.

December 4. The Plain Dealer and the Press
raised the price of their dailies to seven
cents.

December 28. The Detroit Lions defeated the Cleveland Browns, 17-7, for the League Championship.

1953   October 12. Mayor Burke was appointed to the Senate to fill the seat left vacant by the death of Senator Robert A. Taft.

November 3. State Senator Anthony J. Celebreeze was elected Mayor.

1954   September 18. The Indians won the American League pennant.

October 2. The New York Giants won the fourth game, and swept the World Series, defeating the Indians four games to none.

1955   June 3. Four robbers stole $60,000 from the Cleveland Trust Company.

May 29. Mayor Celebreeze named twenty-five citizens to the Cleveland Seaport Foundation to promote the city.

October 5. Mayor Celebreeze won the primary election.

November 5. Mayor Anthony Celebreeze was reelected.

1956   The Cleveland Browns played the College All-Stars in the Chicago _Tribune_ benefit game.

August 19. The _Plain Dealer_ joined the _News_ in the enlarged _News_ building. The papers would continue to operate independently, but with a combined mechanical department.

1957   October 2. Mayor Celebreeze won the primary election.

October 12. Announcement was made of fourteen projects planned as part of the Downtown Cleveland Slum Clearance and Urban Renewal Program.

November. Mayor Celebreeze was reelected.

1958   May 9. Fifteen actors won Ford Foundation grants for a three-year program at the Cleveland Play House.

June 17. Cleveland was named a typical A-
merican City by the United States Junior
Chamber of Commerce.

October 17. The Cleveland Hotel was sold
by the Hotel Corporation of America to the
Sheraton Corporation. It would be called
the Sheraton-Cleveland.

1959   March 27. The Cleveland News, the Plain
Dealer and the Press raised the price of
their dailies from seven to ten cents.

September 23. A gunman and a woman accomplice gained forced entry into the Cleveland
Trust Company when they threatened violence
to the manager's family. The police laid
siege to the building. The gunman shot himself, and his accomplice escaped.

1960   January 23. The News was sold by the Forest
City Publishing Company to Scripps-Howard,
whose management announced it would suspend
publication. It renamed the Press the
Cleveland Press and Cleveland News.

1961   November 7. Mayor Anthony J. Celebreeze
was reelected.

1962   July 14. Mayor Celebreeze was appointed
Secretary of Health, Education and Welfare
by President John F. Kennedy. Anthony
Celebreeze was confirmed July 20. He delayed
his resignation so that the Mayoral primary
could be held at the same time as the other
primaries.

November. Ralph Locher was elected Mayor.

December 6. Ten patrolmen, who were arrested
because of involvement in burglaries, resigned, although they were released because
of insufficient evidence pending a further
probe.

1963   April 26. R. Findley was named Health and
Welfare Director. He was the first black to
hold a high city job.

November 5. Mayor Locher was reelected without opposition. This was believed to be the
first time a mayor of a major United States
city was so selected.

1964

January 29. Pickets demonstrated at the
Britt School, asking for integration of black
children being transported to it from the
overcrowded Hazeldell School in the black
community. The picketing was cancelled on
January 30, when unrully whites threatened
violence.

January 31. Picketing was renewed by civil
rights groups. The Board of Education agreed
to integration of blacks in white public
schools to which they were being transported,
instead of being kept in separate rooms.

April 6. Twenty-one people were held for
picketing the construction sites of three
public schools in the black area. Those
demonstrating claimed that these schools
would result in resegregation of the school
system.

April 7. Rev. Bruce William Klunder, a
whiteman, was crushed trying to stop a bull-
dozer during a demonstration at the construction site of a school in the black area.
The crowd then attacked the driver, who was
arrested by the police.

April 13. The United Freedom Movement in
Cleveland called for a boycott of the schools,
two department stores and the _Press_. William
F. Boyd, the sole black on the Cleveland Board
of Education, urged all children to join the
boycott on April 18. It was 90% effective
on April 20.

1965

April 14. Reverend Paul Younger and Mrs.
Phyllis Jackson accused the antipoverty program directors of a vested interest in pre-
venting the poor from becoming a new political force before a hearing of a subcom-
mittee of the House of Representatives.

November 2. Democratic Mayor Locher was nar-
rowly defeated in an election against black
independent candidate, Democratic State Representative Carl Stokes.

November 19. After a recount showing that
Mayor Locher had won by 2,143 votes, Representative Stokes conceded.

1966

January 5. Mayor Locher, who nearly lost the

election because of the revolt of the black voters, named Clarence L. Gaines, a black, as Public Health and Welfare Director.

June 24. Community Relations Director, Bertram Gardner, and black leaders warned that Cleveland was facing a racial crisis following incidents of racial unrest in areas which included the black ghetto of Hough.

July 18. Rioting broke out in the Negro area of Hough. After two days of disturbances, Governor Rhodes called up 1,500 National Guardsmen.

July 31. The last of the National Guardsmen finally left the Hough district.

August 18. Residents of Hough began a campaign for the recall of Mayor Locher for having failed to carry out his duties.

1967 April 23. City officials adopted a get-tough policy to stop black street gangs involved in acts of vandalism.

May 26. Rev. Dr. Martin Luther King, Jr. announced that he had selected Cleveland as a target for black action during the summer.

June 16. State Representative Carl Stokes announced his second attempt to become the city's first black Mayor.

July 6. Dr. Martin Luther King announced plans for a massive voter registration drive to defeat Mayor Locher.

October 3. Carl Stokes defeated Mayor Locher in the Democratic mayoral primary.

November 7. Carl Stokes was elected the first black mayor of Cleveland.

November 13. Carl Stokes was inaugurated as mayor.

1968 May 1. Mayor Stokes outlined plans for a ten-year $1.5 billion program to reconstruct and redevelop the entire city.

July 23. Snipers fired on police, with automatic weapons, in the black East Side. Gover-

nor Rhodes called up 700 National Guardsmen to help restore order.

July 24. Mayor Stokes ordered the withdraw-
al of all National Guardsmen and white policemen from the East Side, and placed the
area under the control of black policemen,
black Sheriff's deputies and 500 civilizan
recruits.

July 27. Mayor Stokes announced at a news
conference that the crisis had passed.

October 1. Mayor Stokes was ordered to appear in court to answer charges of miscon-
duct filed by the Citizens Committee for
Law Enforcement.

November 6. Cleveland voters approved a
$100,000,000 antipollution bond issue
to clean up the air and water.

1969   May 12. Fred (Ahmed) Evans, a black man, was
convicted of seven counts of first degree
murder, and sentenced to death in the electric chair for killing three policemen and
one civilian in July, 1968 in the East Side
area of Cleveland.

September 30. Mayor Stokes won the Democratic primary.

November 4. Mayor Stokes was reelected by
a narrow margin. He was inaugurated for
his second term November 10.

1970   January 17. Mayor Stokes named Lieutenant
General Benjamin O. Davis, Jr., highest
ranking black in the armed forces, as Public
Safety Director to succeed J. F. McManamen
who had resigned for health reasons. Davis
would be the first black to head the police
and fire departments of a major United States
city.

February 4. Police Chief William P. Ellen-
burg resigned, denying that he had accepted
bribes from an attorney for Detroit Mafia
leaders to shield a Detroit abortion ring.

June 27. Safety Director Davis earned wide-
spread, but not unanimous praise from whites
and blacks for his efforts to control crime

and racial tensions.

July 27. Benjamin Davis, who had resigned as Public Safety Director, maintained that racial unrest was the major problem facing Cleveland.

October 4. The Ethnic Task Force of the Committee on Catholic Community Action proposed the Cleveland Plan, aimed at directing the newly awakened cultural identity among white ethnic Americans into a coalition with the black community.

November 7. Mayor Stokes cut $28 million from the 1971 budget because of the defeat of the proposal for an income tax increase and recreation bond issue. The Mayor indicated that the city would stop hiring policemen and firemen, and would also cut health, sanitation and urban renewal services.

1971   January 4. Mayor Carl Stokes announced the closing of twenty-six Cleveland recreation halls because of the budget crisis. Most of the 500 employees were to be discharged.

February 6. Voters defeated Mayor Stokes' proposal to increase the city income tax. The city then announced various economy moves. Mayor Stokes called for volunteers to help carry on some of the city services.

April 16. Mayor Stokes announced that he would not run for reelection, indicating that he would work to help minority groups throughout the nation.

September 28. J. M. Carney, ex-Representative, won an upset victory in the Democratic mayoral primary. County Auditor Ralph J. Perk was named the Republican nominee. Arnold R. Pinkney, President of the Education Board, announced his intention to run as an independent with the support of Mayor Stokes.

November 2. Ralph J. Perk was elected mayor in an upset victory.

1972   February 12. In an economy move Mayor Ralph J. Perk ordered a ten percent cut in city working hours and pay. This saving of $8 to

$9 million was an attempt to balance the city's proposed 1972 budget.

February 18. Sanitation workers ended a two-day strike under a 14-day restraining order. They had been protesting Mayor Perk's ten percent wage reduction.

February 27. The Ohio Appeals Court over-ruled a lower court refusal to permit the city to reduce the salaries of firemen and policemen by ten percent. Mayor Perk offered to have the two groups vote to see if they would voluntarily accept the reduction. If they refused 561 policemen and firemen would be laid-off.

September 25. Municipal employees went out on strike. Mayor Perk ordered the workers to return to work by October 2 or face legal action. The police and fire departments did not participate although all other city services were at a standstill.

October 2. Teamster Local 244 and the Municipal Foremen and Laborers Local 1099 approved the city's wage offer. The members of the State, County and Municipal Employees Federal Local 100 accepted the wage agreement on October 3. All parties returned to work after this final approval.

November 27. Mayor Ralph J. Perk informed the police department that they had to cut the crime rate by five percent in December if they expected to receive the pay increases due January 1, 1973.

December 23. U. S. District Court Judge William K. Thomas ruled that Cleveland may hire 188 new policemen as long as at least eighteen percent were black or had Spanish surnames.

1973   January 20. Judge Thomas D. Lambros ruled that members of the National Socialist White People's Party, also known as the American Nazi Party, had the right under the First Amendment to wear swastika armbands to City Council meetings. Mayor Perk interpreted this order as applying only to the Council Chamber although several city councilmen indicated their opposition to his decision to have persons wearing the armbands in other parts of City Hall escorted from the building.

January 31. Nonteaching employees of the Cleveland public schools went out on strike in defiance of a court order. Most teachers refused to cross the picket lines. The strike ended on February 4 when a new one-year contract was approved.

April 6. George D. Forbes was elected the first black President of the City Council.

October 11. James M. Carney, who had been nominated for mayor in Cleveland's non-partisan primary, suddenly withdrew from the race, indicating that if Mayor Ralph Perk ran unopposed further polarization of the city would be avoided. The election board refused to permit the Democrats to designate another candidate because the primary had been non-partisan.

October 23. Cuyahoga County Common Pleas Court Judge George McMinagle ruled that a candidate had to be selected to replace James M. Carney in the mayoral election on November 6.

October 26. The Ohio Appeals Court unanimously upheld the lower court decision in regard to the mayoral election. Mrs. M. M. Cotner, a Democrat and City Council Clerk, was named to oppose Mayor Perk.

November 6. Mayor Ralph J. Perk was reelected.

November 28. Mayor Perk announced plans for removal of 1,104 city employees from the payroll on January 1, 1975 as part of the reduction of the projected deficit.

1975   April 12. Cleveland Sanitation workers, members of Teamsters Local 244, went out on strike. They accepted the city's contract offer on May 1 and returned to work.

July 21. Various municipal clerical, technical and blue collar workers, members of the American Federation of State County and Municipal Employees Local 100, began a

strike for higher wages. They accepted a
tentative contract on July 27 and went back
to work.

September 30. Mayor Ralph J. Perk and School
Board President Arnold Pinkney won the city's
non-partisan mayoral primary.

November 4. Mayor Perk was reelected.

December 28. As a result of the United
States Census Bureau's data on migration
from the cities between 1970 and July 1973,
it was shown that Cleveland's population had
dropped below two million. The city was
therefore replace on the list of the fifteen
largest United States cities by Houston.

1976   July 13. Sanford D. Greenberg, who had been
a member of Lyndon Johnson's White House
staff, purchased the Cleveland Coliseum for
$25 million and 440 adjacent acres for $14.5
million.

DOCUMENTS

The documents in this section have been carefully
selected to illustrate the social, political, commercial
and cultural life of Cleveland, and its role in regard
to the trade of the nation during the nineteenth and
twentieth centuries. The most pertinent items from the
ordinances, charters and reports of various agencies and
departments of the city have been chosen in order to
indicate the major changes, which have occurred in the
governance of Cleveland. Of great importance in this
area is the decision of the municipal government to
direct its attention to urban redevelopment after the
difficult years of the Depression and the Second World
War. Description of some of the important reconstruction and improvement projects are included. Obviously
much more could have been included, but the most important documents were selected due to the limited space.

INSTRUCTIONS TO MOSES CLEAVELAND'S PARTY
1796

The Connecticut Company instruc-
ted Cleaveland how he was to conduct himself in leading the expe-
dition to the area, which was to
become Cleveland. The instructions printed below indicate the
intention of the Company.

Source: Colonel Charles Whittlesey. Early History of
Cleveland, Ohio. . . Cleveland, 1867, 187-188.

INSTRUCTIONS OF THE DIRECTORS TO THEIR AGENT.

To MOSES CLEAVELAND, Esq., of the county of Windham,
    and State of Connecticut, one of the Directors
    of the Connecticut Land Company, Greeting:

We, the Board of Directors of said Connecticut Land
Company, having appointed you to go on to said land, as
Superintendent over the agents and men, sent on to survey and make locations on said land, to make, and enter
into friendly negotiations with the natives who are on
said land, or contiguous thereto, and may have any pre-
tended claim to the same, and secure such friendly in-
tercourse amongst them as will establish peace, quiet,
and safety to the survey and settlement of said lands
not ceded by the natives under the authority of the United States. You are hereby, for the foregoing purposes,
fully authorized and empowered to act, and transact all
the above business, in as full and ample a manner as we
ourselves could do, to make contracts in the foregoing
matters in our behalf and stead; and make such drafts on
our Treasury, as may be necessary to accomplish the foregoing object of your appointment. And all agents and
men by us employed, and sent on to survey and settle said
land, to be obedient to your orders and directions. And
you are to be accountable for all monies by you received,
conforming your conduct to such orders and directions
as we may, from time to time, give you, and to do and
act in all matters, according to your best skill and
judgment, which may tend to the best interest, prosperity,
and success of said Connecticut Land Company. Having more
particularly for your guide the Articles of Association
entered into and signed by the individuals of said Company.

/Signed by the Directors/

MOSES CLEAVELAND'S DESCRIPTION OF THE AREA
1796

Moses Cleaveland, founder of the
City of Cleveland, arrived in July, 1796. His description of the
uninhabited land and his meeting
with the Indians indicates how ar-
rangements were made to take over
the territory.

Source: Colonel Charles Whittlesey. Early History of
Cleveland, Ohio. . . Cleveland, 1867, 181-184.

EXTRACT FROM THE JOURNAL OF GENERAL
MOSES CLEAVELAND

On this creek ("Conneaught") in New Connecticut
land, July 4th, 1796, under General MOSES CLEAVELAND,
the surveyors, and men sent by the Connecticut Land Company to survey and settle the Connecticut Reserve, and
were the first English people who took possession of it.
The day, memorable as the birthday of American Independence, and freedom from British tyranny, and commemor-
ated by all good freeborn sons of America, and memorable
as the day on which the settlement of this new country
was commenced, and in time may raise her head amongst the
most enlightened and improved States. And after many
difficulties perplexities and hardships were surmounted,
and we were on the good and promised land, felt that a
just tribute of respect to the day ought to be paid.
There were in all, including men, women and children,
fifty in number. The men, under Captain TINKER ranged
themselves on the beach, and fired a Federal salute of
fifteen rounds, and then the sixteenth in honor of New
Connecticut. We gave three cheers and christened the
place Port Independence. Drank several toasts, viz:
        1st.   The President of the United States.
        2d.   The State of New Connecticut.
        3d.   The Connecticut Land Company.
        4th.   May the Port of Independence and the fifty
sons and daughters who have entered it this day be successful and prosperous.
        5th.   May these sons and daughters multiply in six-
teen years sixteen times fifty.
        6th.   May every person have his bowsprit trimmed and
ready to enter every port that opens.
        Closed with three cheers. Drank several pails of
grog, supped and retired in remarkable good order.
        July 5th.--Wrote letters to the directors and my
wife. Two boats were dispatched under the direction of

TINKER to Fort Erie, to bring the remainder of stores
left there. The Conneaut is now choked with sand. The
stream is capable of admitting boats the greater part of
the year, up beyond the Pennsylvania line, which in a
straight line cannot be more than four miles.

    <u>July 7th</u>.--Received a message from the Paqua Chief
of the Massasagoes, residing in Conneaut, that they
wished a council held that day. I prepared to meet them,
and after they were all seated, took my seat in the mid-
dle. CATO, son of PAQUA, was the orator, PAQUA dictated.
They opened the council by smoking the pipe of peace and
friendship. The orator then rose and addressed me in the
language of Indian flattery, "Thank the Great Spirit for
preserving and bringing me there, thank the Great Spirit
for giving a pleasant day," and then requested to know
our claim to the land, as they had friends who resided
on the land, and others at a distance who would come
there. They wanted to know what I would do with them.
I replied, informing them of our title, and what I had
said to the Six Nations, and also assured them that they
should not be disturbed in their possessions, we would
treat them and their friends as brothers. They then
presented me with the pipe of friendship and peace, a
curious one, indeed. I returned a chain of wampum, silver trinkets, and other presents, and whisky, to the
amount of about twenty-five dollars. They also said they
were poor; and as I had expressed, hoped we should be
friendly and continue to be liberal. I told them I
acted for others as well as for myself, and to be liberal
of others property was no evidence of true friendship;
those people I represented lived by industry, and to
give away their property lavishly, to those who live in
indolence and by begging, would be no deed of charity.
As long as they were industrious and conducted themselves
well, I would do such benevolent acts to them as would
do them the most good, cautioned them against indolence
and drunkeness. This not only closed the business, but
checked their begging for more whisky. . .

CLEVELAND: EARLY 19th CENTURY

Many migrants to the Cleveland area
indicated the primitive aspects of
this region. The descriptions,
written at a later date, illustrate
the wilderness nature, as well as
the opportunities for establishing
families in the town. In addition,
a picture of the early social and
economic life are presented to illustrate the community spirit of
the early settlers.

Source: Samuel P. Orth. A History of Cleveland, Ohio.
. . . Chicago-Cleveland, 1910, vo. I, 414-415, 510;
Col. Charles Whittlesey. Early History of Cleveland,
Ohio. . . . Cleveland, 1867, 416-425.

THOMAS D. WEBB'S DESCRIPTION
OF CLEVELAND IN 1807

I first saw Cleveland in October, 1807. I put up
for a day or two with Major AMOS SPAFFORD, who kept a
tavern. Having a letter of introduction to Governor
HUNTINGTON (then, however, a Judge,) I called at his
house, and as he was absent on the circuit of the Supreme
Court, I presented it to his wife and induced her to
board me for a short time. I remained about three weeks,
I think, and then left Cleveland. GOV. HUNTINGTON then
lived in a log house, standing a little south of Superior
street, not far from the site of the American House. He
had a frame barn, in size thirty feet by forty, near by.
In his barn-yard I saw wild turkies for the first time.
At that time the family of Governor HUNTINGTON was composed of his wife, children, the number I do not recollect, and one female domestic, PATTY RYAN, who came with
him from Connecticut, another, a Miss COBB, who also came
with him, had returned. All the families on the city or
ten acre lots, or the lands adjoining, at that time, that
I recollect, and I think that I recollect all, were,
AMOS SPAFFARD, -- GILBERT, NATHAN PERRY, LORENZO CARTER,
SAMUEL HUNTINGTON, JOHN WALWORTH, and an Irish family
I have forgotten. SAMUEL DODGE had lived on a ten acre
lot, but had at that time take up his residence at Euclid; other families had resided there also, but at the
time I arrived, had removed. There were the remains of
some two or three buildings along the bank of the river,
one of which I was told had been occupied as a store by
a Scotchman, by the name of ALEX. CAMPBELL.
Those buildings were all occupied at that time.
When I was at GOV. HUNTINGTON'S. there was a social party at his house, so far as I recollect, all females, ex-

cept myself. There were several married ladies, I re-
collect particularly but two, Mrs. WALWORTH and Mrs.
HUNTINGTON. We had all, or nearly all, the young ladies
in the place. I think there could not have been more
than one absent; those present were she that is now Mrs.
LONG, Mrs. MATHEWS, of Painesville, and a daughter of
Mr. CARTER, afterwards Mrs. MILES and subsequently Mrs.
STRONG.

R. F. PAINE'S DESCRIPTION OF CLEVELAND, SECOND DECADE OF THE 19th CENTURY

        In 1815, when I was between four and five years old,
my father removed from Richfield county, Connecticut, into
Nelson, Portage county. We left Connecticut in a one-
horse wagon, with hoops drawn over it and cloths spread
over the hoops, and a provision chest of such eatables
as could be got at handily, and in coming from Connecticut to Nelson, Portage county, we were thirty-six days
on the road. Now no conception can be formed of the
privations and hardships those endured that came into
the country as late as that; but several years before
the country had been to some extent settled and the Indians had been driven out from that part of the county
at that time. But they had left plenty of bears and
wolves. I can remember when I no more dared to go out
at night without a brand of fire than nothing. My mother
would not permit nor would my father, nor would I dare
to do it if they would. Every farmer had a little flock
of sheep growing, and every farmer had a pen where he
put them at night and fastened them in, and the pen was
built so high that the wolves could not get into them at
all, and we had fourteen sheep. One night when the
snow was very deep, the wolves came round the pen and
scared the sheep so that eight jumped out and every one
of them lay there in the morning and we had pelts and
mutton plenty for sale, and that would be the case of
every farmer who suffered his sheep to be exposed at
night. And as far as personal safety was concerned I
can remember the daily charge of my mother to my father
when he left home in the morning to be sure to get back
before dark. I remember he went to the center of Nelson
and he wanted to get a tap fixed for sap trees. Mother
kept going to the door and listening and at length we
heard somebody halloo in that direction, and mother said
"Is that father's voice?" Well, we were pretty well
scared. In about three fourths of an hour father came in
leading a big dog by the ear, and the history of his
adventure was that he had got belated within two miles
of home and was treed by two wolves and kept up in the
tree until he hallooed, and a dog that belonged to a man
a half mile away on the other side came up and drove off

the wolves, and father to protect himself took the dog
by the ears and led him home. I recollect one day he
came with a long forked stock with a rattlesnake on it
which he had killed. Now I never had a pair of shoes.
I don't think I had a pair of shoes until I was ten years
old. We wore moccasins made of deer skin. Our house was
a log house of course; the floor was made of split logs
and I have seen them try to dance on them; danced myself
on them. When I would jump on one end the other end
would fly up in your face pretty near. The table was
about as rude, and no child was supposed to sit at table. I stood at the table until I got tall and then they
got me a bench. There were no dishes of any kind scarce-
ly. There was an old fellow by the name of Luke Vokes of
Trumbull county who made wooden dishes and his advent
into the neighborhood with a lot of wooden dishes would
excite more interest than the establishment of another
national bank in the city of Cleveland today. We all
ate on what we called trenchers. They were wooden dishes
like a plate but would wear through after a while; and
the method of serving up meat in those days was to have
a deep dish in the centre of the table, have the meat
cut up into mouthfuls in the frying pan and returned
after being cut up to the spider again and cooked a
little more and turned into this dish in the centre and
every guest at the table had a knife and fork and if he
wanted any meat he must dig it from that dish in the
centre of the table. That was the rude way in which all
lived. The neighbors, so far as I know, were all in the
same condition, using wooden plates, wooden bowls, wooden
everything, and it was years before we could get the
dishes that were any harder than these and when we did,
they were made of this yellow clay.

MALINDA RUSSELL'S REMINISCENCES OF
CLEVELAND, 1812-1814

In 1811 my grandfather, Jacob Russell, sold his
farm and gristmill on the Connecticut river and took a
contract for land in Newburg (now Warrensville) Ohio.
His eldest son, Elijah, my father, shouldered his knap-
sack and came to Ohio to get a lot surveyed; he made
some improvements, selected a place for building and
then returned to New York, where he lived. In the spring
of the following year he with his brother Ralph came a-
gain to Ohio, cleared their piece of land, planted corn,
built a log house and went to Connecticut to assist in
bringing the family to their new home, which was accom-
plished in the Autumn of the same year. Father's brother
Elisha and brother-in-law Hart Risley with their families
accompanied him with their families, the wagons were

drawn by oxen, my father walking all the way so as to
drive, while grandmother rode on horseback. When they
were comfortably settled as might be, father returned to
his family whom he moved the next Summer, 1813, embarking
at Sackett's Harbor, New York, August 1st, and arriving
at Cleveland, August 31st. There being no harbor at that
time the landing was effected by means of row boats. We
then pulled ourselves up the bank by the scrub oaks which
lined it, and walked to the hotel kept by Major Carter;
this hotel was the only frame house in Cleveland. We
staid there over night and next day walked to Rodolphus
Edwards', staid there that night and the next day walked
to grandfather's.

Father was taken sick with ague the next day after
we arrived, so our house was built slowly and with the
greatest difficulty mother hewed with an adz the split
ends of the floor boards and put them down with the little
help father could give her. We moved in the last of November without door or window, using blankets for night
protection. At that time two of the children were sick
with ague. Father worked when the chills and fever left
him for the day putting poles together in the form of
bedsteads and a table upon which we could put the little
we could get to eat, and benches to sit upon; there was
no cabinet shop at that time where such articles could
be purchased.

The only flour we could get had become musty in
shipping and was so disgusting to the taste that no one
could eat it unless compelled by extreme hunger. I was
then eight years old and not sick so I had to satisfy
myself with it and give the others more of a chance at the
scanty corn meal rations. The bread made from this flour
was hard as well as loathsome. I could only eat it by
making it into pellets and swallowing it whole. Toward
the last of February father and one of his brothers started for Aurora, Portage county, with an ox team, taking
an ax, gun and means for camping out. In due time they
arrived, paid ten shillings a bushel for corn and two
dollars and a quarter for wheat, bought an iron kettle
for making sugar and turned their faces homeward. A
glorious surprise awaited them in the woods in the form
of a bee tree from which they obtained nearly a hundred
pounds of honey. Father bought a cow, paid for her in
part and gave his note for the rest and before the time
came to pay again, the cow died, having been in use by
the family only three months. When spring opened father
made sugar, with the help of mother and the children.
In May, mother and three children were taken sick with
ague. Every few days father would have a relapse, but
he managed to get in some corn, and in the autumn some
wheat. Wild meat could be had in abundance.

I remember the bears killed a nice shoat in harvest
time. We were then in need of meat; beef was an article

never spoken of. A man at Doane's Corners had a barrel
of pork to sell, valued at twenty-five dollars. Our
neighbors were also in need of pork and agreed to take
a part if father would go and buy it; he did so. When
the barrel was opened, they were surprised and dismayed
to find only three heads and the ribs and shanks of three
shoats. In the winter of 1814 father's sister started to
return home from Rodolphus Edwards' where she had been
spinning, a distance of two miles through the woods, lost
her way in a snow-path and was out all night and the next
day until evening, when she was found. Her feet were
badly frozen and she was so thoroughly chilled that a
long illness ensued.

I remember the wolves coming into enclosures for
four winters, but the sheepfold was built so high they
could not get over it; they only annoyed us with their
hideous noise. Rattlesnakes were common, and surprised
us often, but only one ever came within six feet of the
house.

DESCRIPTION OF FIRST DANCE
July 4, 1801

The entire party when assembled consisted of fifteen
or sixteen couples. They occupied the front room or par-
lor of the cabin which was not carpeted but had a substantial puncheon floor. The violinist, Mr. Jones, pro-
ceeded at once to harmonize the strings of his instrument and then struck up "Hie Bettie Martin," the favor-
ite dancing tune of that day. The dance commenced with
unrestrained enthusiasm, and with orders to cast off
right and left. The refreshments which had been provided
with a liberal hand, consisted of plum cake and a cordial
of raw whiskey sweetened with maple sugar. The dance
continued until "broad daylight" when the boys went home with the
with the girls in the morning.

The method of courtship in those days was graphi-
cally described by J. D. Taylor at a meeting of the pioneers held at Rockport. "I am reminded of the 'good
old times' and of experiences to which none of the speakers have alluded: I mean pioneer courtships. Topics of
this kind are always interesting, especially to the ladies. Courting, or sparking, in those early days was
not a flirtation but an affair of the heart and conducted in a natural way. The boys and girls who were pre-
disposed to matrimony used to sit up together Sunday
nights dressed in their Sunday clothes. They occupied
usually a corner of the only family room of the cabin,
while the beds of the old folks occupied the opposite
corner, with blankets suspended around it for curtains.
During the earlier part of the evening the old and young
folks engaged in common chitchat. About 8 o'clock the

younger children climbed the ladder to the corner and
went to bed in their bunks under the garret roof, and in
about an hour later father and mother retired behind the
blanket-curtains, leaving the "sparkers" sitting at a
respectful distance apart before a capacious wood fire-
place, looking thoughfully into the cheerful flame or
perhaps into the future. The sparkers, however, soon
broke the silence by stirring the fire with a wooden
shovel or poker, and soon a smack would be heard by the
older people behind the curtains. If chilly the sparkers
would sit closer together to keep warm. All this accords
in a large degree with my own experience.

JULY 4th CELEBRATION, 1818

        July 4, 1818, in Cleveland there was a parade, the
Declaration was read and an oration delivered from a bower
in the Square, and the "Herald" announced that "Immediately after the exercises are over at the courthouse the
gentlemen will again form in order and march to the hotel,
where dinner will be served up and toasts drank, accompanied with the discharging of artillery.
        Of all the days in the year, the Fourth of July, or
Independence day, as it was then called, was the one most
longed for and the longest remembered. It was the grand
holiday of holidays. It was planned for months ahead.
The hoeing was done and the haying never touched until
this memorable day had passed. To these early settlers
it was truly the "glorious Fourth." Many of the pioneers
had taken part in the struggle for independence. It was
nearer to them in point of years than our great Civil
war is to us today. When this day was to be ushered in,
long before the dawn appeared, in East Cleveland, Kil-
berry's old blacksmith's anvil had been fired off by the
boys to wake up the people, and every one was astir
earlier than usual. Several days before, a president of
the day and a committee for various things had been appointed. That everything might be ready, this committee
met the previous day and constructed a bowery in the orchard of Job Doan's tavern, the liberty pole was also
brought from the woods and set up. This orchard of Job
Doan's was used for the Fourth of July celebration for
a good many years. It was directly back of the present
East End postoffice. The bowery was made in the following
fashion: Crotched sticks were stuck into the ground at
regular intervals over a space one hundred feet or so
in length and wide enough to enclose a table with seats
upon either side. The table and seats were made of rough
boards and the top of the bowery was covered with fra-
grant hemlock boughs upon the eventful morning. The
first thing was to raise the flag, and then the jollifi-
cation began.

Baskets were brought and tables were spread with all
the dainties the land could afford. The greatest orna-
ments of the table, however, were the three roast pigs,
each with a corncob in his mouth. One was placed in the
centre of the table and the others at the ends. The rest
of the long board was filled in with rye and corn bread
and a bountiful supply of all the vegetables that we cul-
tivated. The drinks were rye coffee, tea, egg-nog, tod-
dy and whiskey straight. Everybody got mellow; it was
one of the privileges of the day. After dinner the
women folks stored the slights remnants of food in the
Indian baskets and the speechmaking began. Every speech
was impromptu, but I remember such ones as stirred our
souls with enthusiasm.

GEORGE WATKINS' DESCRIPTION OF EARLY
19th CENTURY LOGGING BEE

The day for the bee had been appointed some days
ahead so that the men could arrange their work before-
hand. The men were assembled. They were divided into
two parties and each party had a yoke of oxen. One man
drove, one carried the log chain and four or five rolled
the logs together. The piles were about ten feet high
and bout forty to fifty log heaps were made. Some of
these logs had been chopped, others "niggered." This
process... helped matters. One log was rolled across
another and set on fire when they crossed. This would
burn at night and in its way help along. Of course this
had been done before the logging bee. There was nothing
for the neighbors to do but draw the logs together and
pile them up. There was little market for wood, but
such trees as were thought to be suitable had been drawn
away and cut and split into firewood by the boys. When
the men had finished, the fun began. About sunset the
boys and girls set fire to the heaps. It was the dry
season and the flames leaped and darted over the dry
wood and an immense conflagration was soon well under
way. As soon as the coals appeared. the nearest corn
field was raided for roasting ears. No other corn was
half so sweet as that common field corn roasted by those
blazing fires. The next move was to find a watermelon
patch. After the work was done, the old folks repaired
to the house where the women folks had already assembled,
and ate nut cakes, corn bread and potatoes, and drank
tea, eggnog and whiskey. When the men had drunk enough
to unloose their tongues they talked about the hardships
of men who came to a new country as pioneers before they
could get ready to live. Of the future outcome of their
labor, they entertained bo doubt. These talks were never
in a complaining spirit . . . .

INCORPORATION OF THE VILLAGE OF CLEVELAND
December 23, 1814

Cleveland was first incorporated
as a village on December 23, 1814.
The original charter printed below
stipulated the boundaries, officers
to be elected and their duties, me-
thods of operation, taxing authority and judicial procedures. Officers included a president, recorder,
trustees, treasurer, marshall and
assessors.

Source: <u>Charters of the Village of Cleveland. . .</u> Cleveland, 1851, 5-11.

AN ACT TO INCORPORATE THE VILLAGE OF
CLEVELAND, IN THE COUNTY OF CUYAHOGA

SECTION 1. <u>Be it enacted by the General Assembly</u>
<u>of the State of Ohio</u>, That so much of the city plat of
Cleveland, in the township of Cleveland, and county of
Cuyahoga, as lies northwardly of Huron street, so called,
and westwardly of Erie street, so called, in said city
plat, as originally laid out by the Connecticut Land
Company, according to the minutes of the survey and map
thereof, now on record in the office of the recorder in
said county of Cuyahoga, shall be and the same is hereby
erected into a village corporate, henceforth to be known
and distinguished by the name of "The Village of Cleveland," subject however to such alterations as the legislature may from time to time think proper to make.
SEC. 2. <u>Be it further enacted</u>, That for the better
regulation and government of said village, it shall be
lawful for the electors who shall have been resident in
said village for one year, next preceeding the time or
times of holding elections hereinafter mentioned, to meet
on the first Monday in June next, and on the first Monday
in June annually, thereafter, and elect by ballot a president, recorder, three trustees, a treasurer, village marshal, and two assessors, each of whom at the time of his
election, shall be a freeholder or householder in said
village, and have been a resident therein one year next
preceeding said election; and each of said officers shall,
be a freeholder or householder in said village, and have
been a resident therein one year next preceeding said
election; and each of said officers shall, within five
days after being notified of his election, take an oath
or affirmation before some person authorised to administer the same, faithfully to discharge the duties of his

office, and shall hold such office for one year, and until his successors shall be elected and qualify.

SEC. 3. <u>Be it further enacted</u>, That the first election under the provisions of this act, shall be held at
the court-house in said village, and all subsequent elections at such place as the president shall direct, and all
such elections shall be opened between the hours of 12
and 1 o'clock P. M. and closed at 4 P. M. At the first
election two judges and a clerk shall be appointed viva
voce, by the elctors present, who shall severally take
an oath or affirmation faithfully to discharge the duties
of their respective offices; and at all subsequent elections the president and judges, or any two of them who
shall be present, shall be judges, and the recorder,
clerk of the election; . . .

SEC. 4. Be it further enacted, That the president,
recorder and trustees, and their successors in office, so
as aforesaid elected and qualified, shall be a body politic and corporate, to be known and distinguished by the
name of "The Trustees of the Village of Cleveland;" and
by the name aforesaid shall have perpetual succession,
with the capacity to purchase, receive, hold and convey
any estate, real or personal, for the use of said village: . . .

SEC. 5. <u>Be it further enacted</u>, That the trustees,
or a majority of them, whereof the president or recorder shall always be one, shall have full power and authority to make and publish such laws and ordinances in
writing, and the same from time to time to alter or repeal, as to them shall seem necessary and proper for the
interest, safety, improvement and convenience of said
village; . . .

SEC. 6. <u>Be it further enacted</u>, That the trustees
shall have power to regulate markets, to open and cause
to be kept open, the streets, lanes and alleys of said
village, and to repair and improve the same, to remove
nuisances, to prevent any animals belonging to the inhabitants of said village, from running at large in the
streets, if in their opinion the interest and convenience
of said village shall require such prohibition; to erect
and keep in repair such public buildings or other works
of public utility as may be deemed necessary or useful;
. . .

SEC. 7. Be it further enacted, That upon the petition of twelve freeholders or householders, residents in
said village, and having the qualifications of electors
therein, praying for the establishment of any new street
or streets in said village, describing the same, the
trustees shall have power to lay out, establish and open
such new street or streets so prayed for, and cause a full
and complete record thereof to be made and kept by said
recorder: . . .

SEC. 11. <u>Be it further enacted</u>, That it shall be the

duty of the recorder to make and keep a true and accurate
record of all laws and ordinances made and established, of
streets laid out by the trustees, and of all their proceedings in their corporate capacity, which records shall
at times be opene to the inspection of every elector in
said village; and in case of the absence or disability
of the president, the recorder is hereby authorised and
required to do and perform all the duties of a trustee
and assessor, if elected to both offices.

SEC. 12. _Be it further enacted_, That if any person
or persons shall think himself, herself, or themselves,
aggrieved by any act or judgment of the trustees, it
shall be lawful for such person or persons, within ten
days to appeal to the court of common pleas for the proper
county, who shall hear such causes and or complaints, and
grant such relief as to them may appear necessary and
proper: _Provided_, Such appellant give security, to be
approved of by the clerk of the court to prosecute such
appeal to effect and abide the judgement of the court
thereon.

* * *

CLEVELAND IN 1831

Milo Hickox, who came to Cleveland
from Rochester in 1831, left a
description of the town, which indicates its growth and prosperity.
He points out that living expenses were high, but wages low. He
also tells of problems concerning
health, and in finding household
help.

Source: "Annals Early Settlers Association," vol. 3,
p. 75 in Samuel P. Orth. A History of Cleveland. . .
Chicago-Cleveland, 1910, vol. I, 109.

Cleveland is about two thirds as large as Rochester,
on the east side of the river and is the pleasantest
sight that you ever saw. The streets are broad and cross
each other at right angles. The courthouse is better than
the one in Rochester; the rest of the buildings altoge-
ther, are not worth more than four of the best in that
place and one room of a middling size rents one dollar
per month. Everything that we want to live upon com-
mands cash and a high price. Mechanics' wages are low.
Journeymen get from ten to twenty dollars per month and
board; I get nine shillings and six pence per day and
board myself. There are between fifteen and twenty grog
shops and they all live. There was one opened here last
week by a man from Rochester. There is a temperance society with ten or a dozen male members. The Presbyterian
church has four male members, Baptist six, Methodist a-
bout the same; the Episcopal is small; they have a house,
the others have not. The courthouse is used at this
time for a theatrical company and is well filled with
people of all classes. My health has not been good since
wer have been here. About four weeks since, we awoke in
the morning and found ourselves all shaking with the ague.
I had but one fit myself. My wife had it about a week
every day, and my son three weeks every day, and what made
it worse, my wife and son both shook at the same time.
I spent one day in search of a girl; gave up the chase
and engaged passage for my wife to Buffalo, to be for-
warded to Rochester. She was to leave the next morning.
I was telling my troubles to an acquaintance, who told
me that he would find a girl for me, or let me have his,
rather than have my family leave, so we concluded to
stay.

INCORPORATION OF THE CITY OF CLEVELAND,
March, 1836

Cleveland was made a city in 1836.
The Charter provided for a mayor as
chief executive, and a city council
as the legislative body. The following selection indicates the boundaries at the time, establishment of
three wards, and the duties of
elected officials.

Source: Charters of the Village of Cleveland, and the
City of Cleveland. . . . Cleveland, 1851, 16-19.

AN ACT. TO INCORPORATE THE CITY OF

CLEVELAND, IN THE COUNTY OF CUYAHOGA

PASSED MARCH, 1836

SECTION 1.   Be it enacted by the General Assembly of
the State of Ohio, That so much of the county of Cuyahoga as is contained within the following bounds, viz: Be-
genning at low water mark, on the shore of Lake Erie, at
the most northeastwardly corner of Cleveland ten acre lot
No. 139, and running thence on the dividing line between
lots Nos. 139 and 140, Nos. 107 and 108, Nos. 80 and 81,
Nos. 55 and 56, Nos. 31 and 32, and Nos. 6 and 7, of the
ten acre lots, to the south line of ten acre lots; thence
on the south line of the ten acre lots, to the Cuyahoga
river; thence to the center of Cuyahoga river; thence
down the same to the termination of the west pier; thence
to the township line between Brooklyn and Cleveland;
thence Northwardly to the County line; thence Eastwardly
with said line to a point due North of the place of beginning; thence south to the place of beginning; shall be,
and is hereby declared to be a city; and the inhabitants
thereof are created a body corporate and politic, by the
name and style of "The City of Cleveland;" and by that
name shall be capable of contracting and being contracted
with, of suing and being sued, pleading and being implead-
ed, answering and being answered unto, in all courts and
places, and in all matters whatsoever; with power of pur-
chasing, receiving, holding, occupying and conveying real
and personal estate; and may use a corporate seal, and
change the same at pleasure; and shall be competent to
have and exercise all the rights and privileges and be
subject to all the duties and obligations appertaining
to a municipal corporation.
SEC. 2.   That the government of said city, and the
exercise of its corporate powers, and management of its
fiscal, prudential and municipal concerns, shall be vested

in a Mayor and Council, which Council shall consist of three members from each ward, actually residing therein, and as many Aldermen as there may be wards, to be chosen from the city at large, no two of which shall reside in any one ward, and shall be denominated the City Council; and also such other officers as are hereinafter mentioned and provided for.

SEC. 3. That the said City, until the City Council see fit to increase, alter or change the same, be divided into three wards, in the manner following, to wit; The first ward shall comprise all the territory lying easterly of the center of the Cuyahoga river, and southerly of the center of Superior lane and Superior street to Ontario street, and of a line thence to the center of Euclid street, and of said last mentioned centre. The second ward shall comprise all the territory, not included in the first ward lying easterly of the centre of Seneca street. The third ward shall include all the territory westerly of the centre of Seneca street, easterly of the westerly boundary of the city, and northerly of the center of Superior street and Superior land.

SEC. 4. That the mayor, aldermen, councilmen, marshal and treasurer of said city, shall be elected by the qualified voters thereof, at the annual election of said city, to be held on the first Monday in March, and shall hold their respective offices for one year, and until their successors are chosen and qualified: it shall be the duty of the Mayor to keep the seal of said city, sign all commissions, licenses and permits, which may be granted by the city council; to take care that the laws of the state and the ordinances of the city council be faithfully executed; to exercise a constant supervision and control over the conduct of all subordinate officers, and to receive and to examine into all complaints against them for neglect of duty; to preside at the meetings of the city council when other duties shall permit; to recommend to said council such measures as he may deem expedient; to expedite all such as shall be resolved upon by them; and in general to maintain the peace and good order, and advance the prosperity of the city; . . .

SEC. 5. The members of the city council shall, on the second Monday after each annual election, assemble at their council chamber, or some other suitable place in said city, and elect from their own body, a president to preside in their meetings in the absence of the Mayor; and a majority of all the members shall be a quorum for the transaction of business; the city council shall determine the rules of their proceedings, and keep a journal thereof, which shall be open to the inspection of every citizen; . . .

SEC. 6. That the city council shall have the custody and control of all the real and personal estate, and other corporate property belonging to said city, its pub-

lic buildings, rights and interests; and may make such
orders, regulations and provisions, for the maintenance
and preservation thereof, as they shall deem expedient:
it shall be their duty to regulate the policy of the city, preserve the peace, prevent riots, disturbances and
disorderly assemblages: they shall have authority to appoint watchmen, and prescribe fines and penalties for
their delinquencies: to restrain vagrants or other persons soliciting alms or subscriptions: to suppress and
restrain disorderly and gaming houses, billiard tables,
and other devices and instruments of gaming; to prevent
the vending of liquors, to be drank on any canal boat,
or other place not duly licensed; to prevent and punish
immoderate drinking in any street or other highway of
said city; to abate or remove nuisances; to prevent ba-
thing in any public water within the city; to prevent the
encumbering of any of the streets or highways of the city, in any manner whatever; to provide for clearing the
Cuyahoga river of drift wood and other obstructions, and
to prevent encroachments of any kind thereon, within said
city; to regulate the keeping and carrying of gunpowder
and other combustible materials; to establish, alter and
regulate markets; . . . to regulate all taverns and por-
ter houses, and places where spiritous liquors are
bought and sold by less quantity than one quart; all
houses or places of public entertainment; all exhibitions
and public shows; with exclusive power to grant or re-
fuse licenses thereto, or to revoke the same, and to exact such sum or sums therefor, as they may deem expedient; to establish and settle the boundaries of all
streets or highways of all kinds, within the city, and
prevent or remove encroachments thereon; to prescribe
the bonds and securities to be given by the officers of
the city, for the discharge of their duties, when no provision is otherwise made by law; and further to have
power and authority, and it is hereby their duty, to make
and publish from time to time, all such laws and ordinances as to them may seem necessary to suppress vice, provide for the safety, preserve the health, promote the
prosperity, improve the order, comfort and convenience
of said city, and its inhabitants, and to benefit the
trade and commerce thereof, as are not repugnant to the
general laws of the State: and likewise they shall have
power to regulate wharves and the mooring of vessels in
the harbor; to appoint a harbor master, with the usual
powers, and to prevent fishing lights; and for the violation of any ordinance by them, made by the authority of
this act, the said city council may prescribe any penalty
not exceeding one hundred dollars, and provide for the
prosecution, recovery and collection thereof, or for the
imprisonment of the offender, in case of the nonpayment
of such penalty. . . .

CLEVELAND IN 1846

Henry Howe first visited Cleveland
in 1846. He was impressed with
the location of the city, including its views of the surrounding
area and the layout of the streets.
He also indicated the excellence of
the harbor on Lake Erie, which
helped to make it an important tra-
ding center.

Source: Samuel P. Orth.   A History of Cleveland, Ohio
. . . Cleveland-Chicago, 1910, vol. I, 111.

Excepting a small portion of it on the river it is
situated on a gravelly plane, elevated about one hundred
feet above the lake, of which it has a most commanding
prospect. Some of the common streets are one hundred
feet wide and the principle one, Main street, has the ex-
traordinary width of one hundred and thirty-two feet.
It is one of the most beautiful towns in the Union and
much taste is displayed in the private dwellings and the
disposition of shrubbery. The location is dry and heal-
thy and a view of the meanderings of the Cuyahoga river,
and of the steamboats and shipping in the port, and of
the numerous vessels on the lake under sail, presents
a picture exceedingly interesting from the high shore
of the lake.
Near the center of the place is a public square of
ten acres, divided into four parts by intersecting
streets, well enclosed and shaded with trees.
The harbor of Cleveland is one of the best on Lake
Erie. It is formed by the mouth of the Cuyahoga river
and improved by a pier on either side extending four
hundred and twenty-five yards into the lake, two hundred
feet apart and faced with substantial stone mason work.
Cleveland is the great mart of the greatest grain growing
state in the Union and it is the Ohio and Erie canals
that have made it such, though it exports much by way of
the Welland canal to Canada. It has a ready connection
with Pittsburgh through the Pennsylvania and Ohio canal,
which extends from the Ohio canal at Akron to Beaver
creek, which enters the Ohio below Pittsburgh. The natural advantages of this place are unsurpassed in the
West, to which it has large access by the lakes and the
Ohio canal. But the Erie canal constitutes the principal source of its vast advantages. Without that great
work it would have remained in its former insignificance.

NEW CITY CHARTER, May 3, 1852

The State Legislature passed "An
Act to provide for the organization of cities and incorporated
villages on May 3, 1852." The
government of Cleveland was reorganized under this system. The
provisions for its organization
and officers, as well as the
house of correction, and the powers of the City Council are printed below.

Source: The Acts to Provide for the Organization of Cities and Villages. . .   Cleveland, 1855, 16-17, 36-37,
40-43, 78-79.

AN ACT to provide for the organization of cities
and incorporated villages.

(1.) SECTION I. Be it enacted by the General Assembly of the State of Ohio, That all corporations which ex-
isted when the present constitution took effect, for the
purposes of municipal government, either general or special, and described or denominated in any law then in
force, as cities, towns, villages, or special road districts, shall be, and they are hereby organized into cities, and incorporated villages, with the territorial
limits to them respectively prescribed, or belonging, in
manner following: All such municipal corporations, as
in any such laws are denominated cities, shall be deemed
cities; and those denominated towns, villages or special
road districts, shall be deemed incorporated villages;
to be respectively governed as cities, or incorporated
villages, and in case of the latter, for general or
special purposes, as provided in this act; and all acts
now in force, for the organization or government of any
such municipal corporations, shall be and they are hereby repealed; provided, that such repeal shall not de-
stroy, or bar, any right of property, action, or prosecution, which may be vested, or exist, at the time this
act takes effect. . . .

OF CITIES

(52.) SEC. LVI. The corporate authority of citizens,
organized or to be organized under this act, shall be
vested in one principal officer, to be styled the mayor,
in one board of trustees, to be denominated the city
council, together with such other officers as are in
this act mentioned, or as may be created under its authority.

(53.) SEC. LIX. That the qualified voters of each
ward within the several cities shall, on the first Monday of April, A. D. one thousand eight hundred and
fifty-three, elect, by a plurality of votes, two trustees, who shall be residents of the wards in which they
shall be elected, and who shall at the time be qualified
voters therein; and when the city council elected under
this act shall have been organized, as hereinafter provided, they shall proceed and determine by lot the term
of service of each trustee, so elected, so that one of
the trustees from each ward shall serve for two years,
and the other for the term of one year; and at every
succeeding annual city election, one trustee shall be e-
lected by the qualified voters of each ward shall be e-
possess the qualification hereinbefore required, and
whose term of service shall be two years, so that the
terms of the two trustees of each ward shall always ex-
pire in different years; and the persons thus chosen
shall hold their offices until their successors shall be
elected and qualified. The trustees elected for each
city shall, on the next Monday after their election,
assemble together and organize the city council; a majority of the whole number of trustees shall be necessary
to constitute a quorum for the transaction of business;
they shall be judges of the election, returns, and qualification of their own members; they shall determine the
rules of their proceedings, and keep a journal thereof,
which shall be open to the inspection and examination of
any citizen, and may compel the attendance of absent members, in such manner and under such penalties, as they
shall think fit to prescribe; they shall elect from their
own body, a president, who shall preside at their meetings
during the term for which they shall have been elected,
. . . they shall also appoint, from the qualified voters
of the city, a city clerk, who shall have custody of all
the laws and ordinances of the city, and shall keep a
regular and correct journal of the proceedings of the
council, and shall perform such other duties as may be
required by the ordinances of the city; . . .
(54.) SEC. LX. Each city council shall cause to be
provided for its clerk's office, a seal, in the centre
of which shall be the name of the city, and around the
margin the words "City Clerk," which seal shall be af-
fixed to all transcripts, orders, or certificates, which
it may be necessary or proper to authenticate under the
provisions of this act, or of any ordinance of the city.
                      * * *

OF CITIES OF THE FIRST CLASS

(66.) SEC. LXXII. The qualified voters shall elect
a city marshal, a city civil engineer, a city fire engineer, a city treasurer, a city auditor, a city solici-

tor, police judge, and a superintendent of markets, who
shall hold their offices for two years; each of said officers shall continue in office until his successor is
elected and qualified; and shall have such powers and
perform such duties as are prescribed in this act, or
as may be prescribed by any ordinance of the city, not
inconsistent with this act, and which may not be in-
compatible with the nature of their respective offices.
. . .
        (68.) SEC. LXXIV. The city council shall, by a
general ordinance, direct the number of subordinate officers of the police and watchmen to be appointed; they
shall also provide in addition to the regular watch, for
the appointment of a reserved watch, . . . The duty of
the chief and other officers of police, and of the watchmen, shall be, under the direction of the mayor, and in
conformity with the ordinances of the city, to suppress
all riots, disturbances and breaches of the peace; to
pursue and arrest any person fleeing from justice in
any part of the state; to apprehend any and all persons
in the act of committing any offence against the laws of
the state, or the ordinances of the city, and forthwith
bring such person or persons before the police court, or
other competent authority, for examination; and at all
times diligently and faithfully to enforce all such laws,
ordinances and regulations, for the preservation of good
order, and the public welfare, as the city council may
ordain, . . .
        (69.) SEC. LXXVI. That on the first Monday of April
next, there shall be elected three commissioners; . . .
it shall be the duty of the city commissioners to enforce the ordinances of the city, to superintend the
cleaning and improvement, and the lighting of the
streets, lanes, alleys, market spaces, commons, bridges,
sewers, and landings of the city, and perform such other
duties as the council may by ordinance prescribe; they
shall, with the mayor of said city, and the city civil
engineer, constitute the board of city improvements,
and receive such compensation for their services as the
city council may determine; the board of city improvements shall exercise such powers and perform such duties
in the superintendence and construction of public works,
constructed by authority of the city council, or owned
by the city, as the said council may from time to time
prescribe. . . .

ANNEXATION OF OHIO CITY, March 1, 1854

>   After many disagreements between
>   Ohio City and Cleveland, the ci-
>   tizens of the two cities decided
>   that it would be advantageous to
>   merge. The issue was submitted
>   to the voters. In Cleveland the
>   vote was 1892 Yeas to 400 Nays;
>   in Ohio City the vote was 618
>   Yeas to 258 Nays. A portion of
>   the terms of annexation printed
>   below indicates the manner in
>   which the merger was to take place.

Source: The Acts to Provide for the Organization of Cities. . . Cleveland, 1855, 88-91.

TERMS OF ANNEXATION

   This memorandum of an agreement made this 5th day
of June, A. D. 1854, by and between W. A. OTIS, H. V.
WILLSON, and F. T. BACKUS, as Commissioners appointed by
the city council of the city of Cleveland, and W. B. CAS_
TLE, N. M. STANDART, and C. L. RHODES, as Commissioners
appointed by the city council of the city of Ohio, to
arrange the terms and conditions of the annexation of
the said city of Ohio to the said city of Cleveland, in
pursuance of the vote taken in that behalf, by said cities respectively, at the annual election held therein,
on the first Monday in April last, Witnesses--that said
Commissioners, the former acting in behalf of said city
of Cleveland, and the latter acting in behalf of said
city of Ohio, have agreed upon the following terms and
conditions upon which such annexation shall take place,
to wit:
   I.   The territory now constituted the city of Ohio,
shall be annexed to and constituted a part of the city
of Cleveland, and the first, second, third, and fourth
wards of the former city, as now established, shall constitute the eight, ninth, tenth, and eleventh wards, respectively, of the last named city, and the present trustees of said eighth, ninth, tenth, and eleventh wards
of said city of Cleveland, respectively, for the terms
for which they have been severally elected as such trustees of said first, second, third, and fourth wards, but
the boundaries of said wards may be changed, or the number thereof may be increased or diminished, subject to
the provisions contained in the next following article.
   II. The number of wards into which the territory so
annexed shall be divided, shall not, before the first
Monday of April, A. D. 1858, bear a less ratio to the
whole number of wards into which said united city of

Cleveland shall be divided, than four to eleven; nor
shall such number ever bear a less ratio to the whole
number of wards in the city of Cleveland, than the population of such territory shall bear to that of the whole
city.

  III. All the assets, both real and personal, owned
by, or in any manner belonging to the said city of Ohio,
shall vest in, and become the property of said city
of Cleveland, to be held by the latter for the purposes
contemplated in the original acquisition of the same by
the said city of Ohio, but with the same power of disposal over them, as though the same had been originally
acquired for the like purposes by the said city of
Cleveland.

  IV. All the assets, both real and personal, other
than railroad stocks, and rights growing out of the same,
owned by, or in any manner belonging to the city of
Cleveland, as now constituted, shall be the property of
said united city, to be held for the purposes contemplated in the original acquisition, but with the same power
of disposal over the same, as though they had been originally acquired for the like purposes, by said united
city of Cleveland.

  V. That the outstanding debts and liabilities of
every kind, of the said city of Ohio, including the a-
mount to be paid for the purchase of water lot number
eighteen, as authorized by said city council, and those
of the said city of Cleveland, other than such as have
been incurred by the latter, by way of subscriptions to
railroad stocks, shall be provided for and liquidated
by the said united city of Cleveland.

  VI. All railroad stocks now held by the city of
Cleveland, and all rights growing out of the ownership
thereof, shall be, and remain the exclusive property of
that portion of the territory of such united city, which
now constitutes the city of Cleveland, the avails of which
shall be applied to the extinguishment of the liabilities
of said city of Cleveland, heretofore incurred by subscriptions to railroad stocks, and the issue of bonds or
other liabilities of said city of Cleveland, in payment
of such subscription. . . .

THE BOARD OF HEALTH, 1880

There had been differing opinions
concerning the type and make up
of the Board of Health that
should be established in the city。
The original Board of Health had
been established on January 10,
1856. It was abolished in 1876,
and reestablished in 1880. It
was considered to be a necessary
adjunct to the regulation of
city affairs.

Source: Ordinances of the City of Cleveland. Revised and
conolidated by H. L. Vail and L. M. Snyder. Cleveland,
1890, 14-17 and 36-39.

SUBDIVISION I. THE BOARD, ITS POWERS AND DUTIES.

SEC. 37. The powers and jurisdiction in regard to
matters of public health and sanitary affairs shall be
vested in and exercised by a Board of Health, consisting
of the Mayor and six members, to be appointed by the
Council, and have the powers given by Chapter I, Division 6, and Title 12 of the Revised Statues of Ohio.
SEC. 38. The Board of Health shall have power to
abate and remove all nuisances within the city, and assess
the cost and expense of the same upon the property wherein such nuisance is situated, which assessment, when duly
certified by the President of the Board to the County Auditor, shall become a lien, to be collected the same as
any other tax in favor of the city; and to compel the pro-
prietors or owners, agents or assignees, occupants or
tenants of the lot or property, house or building, or o-
ther place in or on which any nuisance may be, to abate
and remove the same.
SEC. 39. Said Board shall have power to regulate the
construction, arrangement, and location of all water clo-
sets, privies, and privy vaults within the city, and the
emptying and cleaning of the same.
SEC. 40. Said Board shall have power to create and
compile an acurate system of registration of births,
deaths and interments occurring in the city, for the purpose of legal and genealogical investigation, and to furnish facts for statistical, scientific and particularly
for sanitary inquiries.
SEC. 41. Said Board shall have power, when complaint
is made, or reasonable belief exists, that any dangerous
infectious or contagious disease exists in any locality
or house to visit such locality or house, make all necessary investigations by inspection and on discovering that
such dangerous infectious or contagious disease exists,

to send the person or persons so diseased to the pest
house or hospital, and if necessary to disperse the inhabitants of such house or locality. . . .

SEC. 47. It shall be the duty of the Health Officer, under the direction and control of said Board, to
enforce all laws, ordinances and regulations relating to
causes of sickness, nuisances and sources of filth existing within the city.

SEC. 48. He may, with the consent of the Board, order any furniture, clothing, or other property, either
to be destroyed, removed or disinfected, whenever he may
deem it necessary for the health of the city.

SEC. 49. He may remove out of the city any person
who is not a resident thereof, and who is supposed to be
infected with any dangerous malignant, contagious, infectious, or pestilential disease, or to the city hospital
or pest house, when he shall deem such removal necessary
to prevent the spread of such diseases, and that such
removal can be made without danger to the life of such
person.

SEC. 50. Whenever the Health Officer shall ascertain that a nuisance affecting or endangering, in his
opinion, the public health, exists on any premises, or
in any house, manufactory, workshop, or other place within the city, he shall notify in writing any person or
persons owning, leasing, occupying, having control of,
or acting as agent for such premises, house, manufactory,
workshop, or place, to abate and remove such nuisance
within a reasonable time, to be stated in such notice,
or in case of necessity the same may be abated or removed
by the Health Officer without such notice.

* * *

District Physicians

SEC. 53. The said Board shall appoint District Physicians in number as it may deem proper, whose duties it
shall be to give free attendance, both medical and surgical to all the destitute poor in their several districts
who shall at any time call upon or send for them. They
shall keep office hours daily, except Sundays, in such
number and at such places as the Board shall from time
to time appoint, and they shall vaccinate all persons in
their several districts who shall call upon them at their
offices, who are unable to pay for the same, and shall
perform any other medical or surgical services in their
several districts required of them by said Board of Health
Officer. They shall hold their Offices at the pleasure
of the Board and shall receive such compensation for their
services as said Board shall from time to time determine.
They shall report to said Board as often as it shall see
fit to command them, the number of cases treated by them
in their several districts, which report shall mention

the nativity, age, sex, color, occupation, social relation, the number of prescriptions and visits made in each
case, the length, cause and name of the disease, the
number of deaths and recoveries occurring in the several
districts since their last report. . . .

RULES AND REGULATIONS OF THE BOARD OF HEALTH

SEC. 141. The following rules and regulations a-
dopted by the Board of Health are hereby approved by
the City Council.

RULE I. No child from any family in which a case of
scarlet fever or diphtheria now exists or may hereafter
occur, shall attend any school in this city, unless con-
valescence in such case shall have been thoroughly established. In all such cases the attending physician shall
certify in writing that this rule has been complied with,
the certificate to be presented to the teacher of the
school before the child is readmitted.

RULE II. In every case where death has occurred
from scarlet fever or diphtheria, the body of the deceased shall be thoroughly disinfected and inclosed in a
tight burial case, which shall not thereafter be opened.
The funeral of such person shall be strictly private, and
in no case shall children be allowed to attend the same;
and the room in which the deceased person was, and the
clothing and bedding used during the sickness, shall be
thoroughly disinfected.

RULE III. The body of no person who may have died
of small-pox, scarlet fever, diphtheria, or other dangerous contagious, pestilential or infectious disease,
shall be removed in a carriage or other conveyance used
by the public.

RULE IV. In the care and burial of all bodies of
persons dying from small-pox, diphtheria or scarlet fever, it shall be the duty of the undertaker, or other
person acting as such, to place every such body within
the casket in which it is to be buried, within six hours
after being first called upon to take charge of the same,
the casket then to be closed and not again opened. It
shall also be the duty of the undertaker, or other person
taking charge of any funeral services, where the corpse
is that of a person dying from small-pox, diphtheria
or scarlet fever, to furnish or provide for such funeral
not more than three two-horse carriages, besides a hearse,
and publicly notify all persons attending such funeral
of the name and contagious character of the disease from
which the person has died.

RULE V. All funeral services held in connection
with the burial of the body of any person dying from
small-pox, diphtheria or scarlet fever, must be private,
including only the nearest family relatives and other
adult persons not exceeding six in number, the head of

the family to be held responsible for the observance of
this rule.

RULE VI. The body of any person dying from small-
pox, diphtheria or scarlet fever, must in no instance be
taken into any church or chapel for funeral services.

RULE VII. No person, company or corporation shall
remove, or cause to be removed, or transport or handle
the contents of any privy vault within the City of Cleveland, without a permit to remove the same is first obtained from the Health Officer. . . .

ESTABLISHMENT OF CASE INSTITUTE, 1880

Leonard Case, one of the more prominent citizens of Cleveland, was
determined to apply his philanthropic endeavors to the establishment
of an institution devoted to tech-
nological studies. The articles
of incorporation indicating the
goals of the institution illustrate the outcome of Mr. Case's
proposal.

Source: Samuel P. Orth. A History of Cleveland, Ohio.
. . Chicago-Cleveland, 1910, vol. I, 106.

ARTICLES OF INCORPORATION.

Whereas Leonard Case, late of the city of Cleveland,
now deceased, in his lifetime conveyed and assured to
Henry G. Abbey, by deeds dated February 24, 1877, and
October 16, 1879, certain real estate therein described,
and upon the limitations, conditions and trusts therein
fully expressed, and thereby directed the said Henry G.
Abbey, immediately upon his death, to cause to be formed
and regularly incorporated under the laws of Ohio, an
institution of learning, to be called "The Case School
of Applied Science," located in said city of Cleveland,
in which should be taught, by competent professors and
teachers, mathematics, physics, engineering--mechanical
and civil--economic geology, mining and metallurgy, natural history, drawing and modern languages; and immediately upon the regular organization of such corporation
to convey by sufficient deed in fee simple, and free and
clear of all encumbrances whatever, the said premises to
such corporation, to be held and enjoyed by it in per-
petuity for the sole and only purpose of collecting and
receiving the rents, issues, and profits thereof, and
applying the same, or the proceeds of said property, to
the necessary cost and expenses of providing for and
carrying forward in a thorough and efficient manner the
teaching above named; and such other kindred branches of
learning as the trustees of said institution should
deem advisable, and to the payment of such other cost and
expenses as might be necessary for the general uses and
purposes of such an institution; and,
Whereas, the said Henry G. Abbey duly accepted the
said trust so confided to him, and has, in conformity with
his own obligations thereunder, caused this instrument and
act to be prepared for execution by himself and his associates therein. . . .

ARTICLES OF INCORPORATION:

Article 1. The name of this corporation shall be "The Case School of Applied Science."

Art. 2. The said corporation shall be located in the city of Cleveland, in the county of Cuyahoga and state of Ohio.

Art. 3. The purpose for which said corporation is formed is to receive a conveyance of property described in the above-mentioned deeds; and by the use of rents, issues, profits and proceeds thereof, organize, establish and maintain in said city of Cleveland, an institution of learning in conformity with the terms of the above-mentioned and recited trust, and to hold and apply for the same uses and purposes any other funds or property lawfully acquired by the corporation. . . .

CITY CHARTER, 1914

The city revised its self-government procedure, and followed the
practice of greater democratic
procedure, by introducing the Recall, Initiative and Referendum.
The selections illustrate the determination to have city officials
responsive to the needs of the
inhabitants.

Source: The Charter of the City of Cleveland bound in
Journal of the First Charter Commission of Cleveland.
Cleveland, 1913, 1, 4-5, 9, 19-22.

THE CHARTER OF THE
CITY OF CLEVELAND

General Powers of the City.
    Section 1. The inhabitants of the City of Cleve-
land, as its limits now are, or may hereafter be, shall
be a body politic and corporate by name "The City of
Cleveland," and as such shall have perpetual succession;
may use a corporate seal, may sue and be sued; may acquire property by purchase, gift, devise, appropriation,
lease, or lease with privilege to purchase, for any municipal purpose; may sell, lease, hold, manage, and control such property, and make any and all rules and regulations by ordinance or resolution which may be required
to carry out fully all the provisions of any conveyance,
deed, or will, in relation to any gift or bequest, or
the provisions of any lease by which it may acquire property; may acquire, construct, own, lease and operate and
regulate public utilities; may assess, levy, and collect
taxes for general and special purposes on all the subjects
or objects which the City may lawfully tax; may borrow
money on the faith and credit of the City by the issue or
sale of bonds or notes of the City; may appropriate the
money of the City for all lawful purposes; may create,
provide for, construct, regulate and maintain all things
of the nature of public works and improvements; may levy
and collect assessments for local improvement; may license and regulate persons, corporations and associations engaged in any business, occupation, profession or
trade; may define, prohibit, abate, suppress and prevent
all things detrimental to the health, morals, comfort,
safety, convenience and welfare of the inhabitants of
the City, and of all nuisances and causes thereof; may
regulate the construction, height, and the material used
in all buildings, and the maintenance and occupancy
thereof; may regulate and control the use, for whatever
purposes, of the streets and other public places; may

create, establish, abolish and organize offices and fix
the salaries and compensations of all officers and em-
ployes; may make and enforce local, police, sanitary and
other regulations; and may pass such ordinances as may
be expedient for maintaining and promoting the peace,
good government and welfare of the City, and for the
perfomance of the functions thereof. . . .

Recall Elections
        Section 9. Any elective officer provided for in
this Charter may be removed from office by the electors
qualified to vote for a successor to such officer. The
procedure to effect such removal shall be as follows:
        (a) A petition, demanding that the question of re-
moving such officer be submitted to the electors qualified to vote for his successor, shall be addressed to the
Council and filed with the Clerk thereof. Such petition
shall be signed by at least fifteen thousand (15,000)
electors, if seeking the removal of an officer elected
from the City at large, and by at least six hundred (600)
electors if for the removal of an officer elected from
a ward.
        (b) The signatures to such petitions need not all be
appended to one paper. Petition papers shall be pro-
cured only from the Clerk of the Council, who shall keep
a sufficient number of such blank petition papers on file
for distribution as herein provided.
        Prior to the issuance of any such blank petition
papers an affidavit shall be made by one or more qualified electors and filed with the Clerk, stating the name
of the officer sought to be removed. The Clerk, upon
issuing any such petition paper to an elector, shall enter, in a record to be kept in his office, the name of
the elector to whom issued, and shall certify upon each
such paper the name of the elector to whom issued and
the date of issuance. No petition paper so issued shall
be accepted as part of a petition unless it bears such
certificate of the Clerk, and unless filed as provided
herein.
        (c) Each signer of a petition shall sign his name in
ink or indelible pencil and shall place thereon, after
his name, his place of residence by street and number.
To each such petition paper there shall be attached an
affidavit of the circulator thereof, stating the number
of signers to such part of the petition and that each
signature appended to the paper was made in his presence
and is the genuine signature of the person whose name it
purports to be.

INITIATIVE AND REFERENDUM.
The Initiative.
        Section 28. Any proposed ordinance may be submitted
to the Council by petition signed by at least five thou-

sand (5,000) qualified electors of the City. The procedure in such cases shall be as follows:

(a) Petitions submitting proposed ordinances to the
Council shall be filed with the Clerk of the Council.
Signatures to such a petition need not all be appended
to one paper but all petition papers, circulated with
respect to any proposed ordinance, shall be uniform in
character and shall contain the proposed ordinance in
full, and have printed thereon the names and addresses
of at least five electors who shall be officially regard-
ed as filing the petition and shall constitute a committee of the petitioners for the purposes hereinafter named.

(b) Each signer of a petition shall sign his name
in ink or indelible pencil, and shall place on the petition paper after his name his place of residence by
street and number. The signatures to any such petition
paper need not all be appended to one paper but to each
such paper there shall be attached an affidavit by the
circulator thereof stating the number of signers to such
part of the petition and that each signature appended to
the paper is the genuine signature of the person whose
name it purports to be, and was made in the presence of
the affiant.

(c) All papers comprising a petition shall be assembled and filed with the Clerk of the Council as one instrument. Within twenty (20) days from the filing of
a petition the Clerk shall ascertain whether it is signed
by the required number of qualified electors. Upon the
completion of his examination the Clerk shall endorse
upon the petition a certificate of the result thereof.

(d) If the Clerk's certificate shows that the petition is insufficient he shall at once notify each member of the committee of the petitioners, herinbefore provided for, and the petition may be amended at any time
within fifteen (15) days from the date of the Clerk's
certificate of examination, by filing with the Clerk
an additional petition paper or papers in the same manner
as provided for the original petition. Upon the filing
of such an amendment the Clerk shall, within ten (10)
days thereafter, examine the amended petition and attach
thereto his certificate of the result. If still insufficient, or if no amendment shall have been filed, the
Clerk shall file the petition in his office and shall notify each member of the committee of that fact. The final
finding of the insufficiency of a petition shall not
prejudice the filing of a new petition for the same purpose.

(e) When the certificate of the Clerk shows the petition to be sufficient, he shall submit the proposed ordinance to the Council at its next regular meeting and
the Council shall at once read and refer the same to an
appropriate committee, which may be the committee of the
whole. Provision shall be made for public hearings upon

the proposed ordinance before the committee to which it
is referred. Thereafter the committee shall report the
proposed ordinance to the Council, with its recommendations thereon, not later than the third regular meeting
of the Council following that at which the proposed ordinance was submitted to the Council by the Clerk.

(f) Upon receiving the proposed ordinance from the
committee, the Council shall at once proceed to consider
it and shall take final action thereon within thirty (30)
days from the date of such committee report. If the
Council reject the proposed ordinance or pass it in a form
different from that set forth in the petition, the committee of the petitioners may require that it be submitted to a vote of the electors in its original form, or
that it be submitted to a vote of the electors with any
proposed change, addition or amendment, which was presented in writing either at a public hearing before the
committee to which such proposed ordinance was referred,
or during the consideration thereof by the Council.

(g) When an ordinance proposed by petition is to
be submitted to a vote of the electors the committee of
the petitioners shall certify that fact and the proposed
ordinance to the Clerk of the Council within ten (10)
days after the final action of such proposed ordinance
by the Council.

(h) Upon receipt of the certificate and the certified copy of the proposed ordinance, the Clerk shall
certify the fact to the Council at its next regular
meeting. If an election is to be held not more than six
months nor less than thirty (30) days after the receipt
of the Clerk's certificate by the Council, such proposed
ordinance shall then be submitted to a vote of the electors. If no such election is to be held within the time
aforesaid the Council may provide for submitting the
proposed ordinance to the electors at a special election.
If a supplemental petition, signed by five thousand
(5,000) qualified electors, in addition to those who
signed the original petition be filed with the Clerk asking that the proposed ordinance be submitted to the voters at a time indicated in such petition, the Council
shall provide for a special election at such time. The
sufficiency of any such supplemental petition shall be
determined, and it may be amended, in the manner provided
for original petitions for proposing ordinances to the
Council. If no other provision be made as to the time
of submitting a proposed ordinance to a vote of the
electors, it shall be submitted at the next election.

(i) The ballots used when voting upon any such proposed ordinance shall state the title of the ordinance to
be voted on and below it the two propositions, "For the
Ordinance" and "Against the Ordinance." Immediately at
the left of each proposition there shall be a square in
which by making a cross (X) the voter may vote for or

against the proposed ordinance.

(j) If a majority of the qualified electors voting on any such proposed ordinance shall vote in favor thereof, it shall thereupon become an ordinance of the City.

(k) Proposed ordinances for repealing any existing ordinance or ordinances in whole or in part may be submitted to the Council as provided in this section.

(l) Ordinances adopted as provided in this section shall be published and may be amended or repealed by the Council as in the case of other ordinances.

The Referendum.

Section 29. No ordinance passed by the Council, unless it be an emergency measure, shall go into effect until forty (40) days after its passage by the Council.

(a) If, at any time, within said forty (40) days a petition signed by electors equal in number to ten per cent (10%) of the total vote cast at the last preceding regular municipal election of the City be filed with the Clerk of the Council requesting that any such ordinance be repealed or submitted to a vote of the electors, it shall not become operative until the steps indicated herein have been taken.

(b) When such a petition is filed with the Clerk of the Council he shall determine the sufficiency thereof in the manner as provided in Section 9 of this Charter. If the petition be found sufficient, or be rendered sufficient by amendment as provided in Section 28 hereof, the Clerk shall certify that fact to the Council, which shall proceed to reconsider the ordinance. If, upon such reconsideration, the ordinance be not entirely repealed, the Council shall provide for submitting it to a vote of the electors, and in so doing the Council shall be governed by all the provisions of Section 28 hereof respecting the submission of ordinances proposed to the Council by petition.

(c) If when submitted to a vote of the electors any such ordinance be not approved by a majority of those voting thereon, it shall be deemed repealed.

(d) Referendum petitions need not contain the text of the ordinances, the repeal of which is sought, but they shall be subject in all other respects to the requirements for petitions submitting proposed ordinances to the Council. . . .

CITY MANAGER FORM OF GOVERNMENT

The interest stimulated by this
form of government is evidenced
in this report of the Cleveland
Real Estate Board which summar-
izes the view points of various
representative elements of the
population. The City Manager
form of government was insti-
tuted in 1923.

Source: The Cleveland Real Estate Board on "Report of the
City Manager Plan Committee."

The one fundamental problem to be worked out in our
political system is how to make democratic government
more efficient. How can liberty and government be har-
monized? The European war is a conflict between the
democracy of England and the autocracy of Germany. These
systems are fighting for worldwide supremacy. However
we (are) may criticize German autocratic systems and the
submerging of the individual in the state; we must admit
that German cities have more liberty than the American.
The world has admired the marvelous efficiency and co-or-
dination of the German people into one mighty industrial
and military unit.

Democratic England was weak and unprepared for the
war but she has been revolutionized. The conflict is
certain to make Russia more democratic and it will bind
together England and her colonies into a greater world
power. All European nations will be more efficiently
integrated in the competition for the world's trade. We
cannot escape the far reaching effect of it all. We are
faced with new conditions, we must see to it that in our
national and local governments we learn how to administer
our laws as well as how to make them. We must do both
with the least waste of time and money.

                      * * *

No private interest must dominate the interest of
all. Individual welfare grows apace with the common welfare. We must have a strong hand to do things if we need
clear heads to determine what should be done. We must
curb selfish private interests by public spirit and good
will and check selfish partisan tyranny be alert and pa-
triotic citizenship. We must balance the centripetal and
centrifugal forces, the citizens must be alive to the
common interests and the community to private interests.

We must think more in our local elections as Clevelanders and less than Democrats and Republicans. We need
a uniting spirit. The fight in our municipal council for
political advantage along national lines should stop. We
should authorize one man, a man of business sense to carry

out policies but not play politics. Let him employ ex-
perts and keep them employed as long as they make good.
. . .

"No, I do not believe city affairs are so administered in any large city (with few exceptions). It is
inevitable that they cannot be administered so. People
generally, in this country, consider the management of
this city a side issue to which they want to give as
little attention as possible. Result Men of experience,
business training and efficiency do not aspire to the position which the city offers. City management should be
a professional and efficiency should assure permanency.
No such conditions exist. Some progress has been made
but until party politics is eliminated and permanency
assured as a result of faithful and efficient choice,
your men are not going to make it a profession and yet it
offers one of the finest fields of endeavor." . . .

The president of a corporation, deliberate and care-
ful in his judgments, says:
"It seems to me that partisanship is the worst enemy
of efficiency in business management. When a recent republican administration came in, they threw out of office
hundreds of men who had spent two years or more in learning their jobs and in whom the city had invested hundreds
of dollars in educating them to the point where they were
when dismissed. It is quite likely that if the next administration is democratic, the process will be repeated.
No private concern could possibly stand this sort of
thing and it is remarkable that the city's work is done
as well as it is, not that it is done as poorly as it is."

An editor writes:
"Yes, criticism is perhaps largely as to streets,
good. We are weary of the subverting of the city's welfare to the private political ambition of any man. We
should give a city manager the power and authorities to
get results. The mandate must be businesslike. It is
ridiculous to offer as an excuse for the partisan game:
'Democrats are kicking now and the Republicans kicked
before'."

Fellow members, it looks as if the Real Estate Board
must help to raise the standard in Cleveland of the more
powerful and economical system. It is a movement for
business men and the people must be educated to it. O-
ther organizations are ready to take action in favor of
the system. We suggest that we join with other civic
bodies and organize a larger committee to make a fuller
research of the results in cities where this plan is in
effect and a more thorough investigation of the results
here.

Your committee is persuaded after five months of study and conference that this plan impracticable in a city
as large as Cleveland. Springfield, Mass. is vigorously
agitating adoption of it. The president of the Boston

City Council has declared in favor of it for that city.
Mayor Blankenburg of Philadelphia whose judgment is entitled to a great weight on account of his long experience
in and study of municipal affairs has recommended this
plan for his city.

We shall have a new profession. We shall be free to
employ the best man to direct our business affairs, no
matter where he may be found, because the common welfare
is just as important as individual welfare.

Cleveland must go to the front. If it is the best
form let us find it out. Shall we nurse our dissatisfac-
tion and refusing to believe in ourselves, permit more
enterprising cities to pass us on the way to progress
and power?

We sent out questionaires - eight questions in all.
Hundreds of replies were made. They are highly representative both of the employed and the employers, the profes-
sions and business men. A large percentage have held
public office, quite a number are men of national repu-
tation. Almost all the answers were given in the spirit
of non-partisanship, these papers are confidential. We
shall quote from them without indicating the name of the
writers. A very large number praise Cleveland in compari-
son with other cities.

Question No. 1 "Do you believe city affairs are being
economically and efficiently administered?"
11 percent voted yes. . . .

A prominent business man says:

"The fact that the Commission Manager plan has been
announced a success by those cities which have adopted
it, is, I believe, sufficient reason for me to answer this
question in the affirmative. Furthermore, if the right
salary is paid and the position is made permanent so
long as efficiency is given I believe that men of high
caliber might be induced to consider accepting a position as Manager.

The president of a large corporation says:

"The city manager plan would tend to prevent the
turning out of hundreds of partially well trained men to
make room for men of no training and, therefore, it seems
to men that it is a plan which should be advocated at
the present time.

The Assistant Manager of a manufacturing concern:

"Yes, but I believe that the future will see us more
nearly approaching the German plan in which the manager
of a city of 5,000 is promoted, if he show capability to
become the manager of a city of 25,000 and so on, until
he perhaps is regraduated into running the largest of
German cities.

One whose name is well known as a public spirited
and generous citizen of Cleveland, says:

"I believe that any plan is desireable which puts
the business administration of the city in the hands of

one man, not subject to the necessity of securing his
re-election at frequent intervals or to the authority
of officials who are so subject. The greatest difficulty with this plan, is that of securing a man with the experience and breath of view essential to the proper
handling of city problems."

From a large garment manufacturer:

"Yes, because a manager would hold his job pending
good service without the fear of losing his job in say
two years. His experience would be culminative and
therefore, more and more valuable to the city."

A prominent attorney who has studied the city manager plan in Dayton and elsewhere:

"Make a more permanent government, tending to eliminate shifting of and changing of employees. Tend to
eliminate politics in appointments. Secure efficiency
in administration by appointment of trained men to run
the city's affairs. . . .

CITY CHARTER, November 3, 1931

The City Charter now in effect was
originally adopted at the general
election of November 2, 1915, a-
mended at the election of November
28, 1921, and amended again at the
election of November 3, 1931. The
selections chosen illustrate the
powers of government, conduct of
referendums and elections, and the
various executive organs, including
the Mayor, the City Planning Commission and the Board of Zoning
Appeals.

Source: The Charter and Codified Ordinances of the City
of Cleveland. Cleveland, 1951, 2-5, 8-11.

THE CHARTER OF THE CITY OF CLEVELAND

CHAPTER 1

SECTION 1. General Powers
The inhabitants of the City of Cleveland, as its limits now are, or may hereafter be, shall be a body politic and corporate by name the City of Cleveland, and as
such shall have perpetual succession; may use a corporate seal; may sue and be sued; may acquire property in
fee simple or lesser interest or estate by purchase,
gift, devise, appropriation, lease, or lease with privilege to purchase, for any municipal purpose; . . . may
acquire, construct, own, lease and operate and regulate
public utilities; may assess, levy, and collect taxes for
general and special purposes on all the subjects or objects which the city may lawfully tax; may borrow money
. . .; may appropriate the money of the city for all lawful purposes; may create, provide for, construct, regulate and maintain all things of the nature of public
works and improvements; . . .The city shall have all powers that now are, or hereafter may be granted to munici-
palities by the constitution or laws of Ohio; and all
such powers whether expressed or implied, shall be exercised and enforced in the manner prescribed by this
charter, or when not prescribed herein, in such manner
as shall be provided by ordinance or resolution of the
Council.
SEC. 2. Enumeration of Powers Not Exclusive.
The enumeration of particular powers by this charter
shall not be held or deemed to be exclusive but, in addition to the powers enumerated herein, implied thereby
or appropriate to the exercise thereof, the city shall
have, and may exercise all other powers which, under the

constitution and laws of Ohio, it would be competent for
this charter specifically to enumerate. . .

SEC. 16.   Removal of Mayor, Member of Council;
Affidavit; Petition.

The Mayor or any member of the council may be removed from office by the electors. The procedure for
effecting such a removal shall be as follows:

Any elector may make and file with the clerk of
the council an affidavit stating the name of the officer
whose removal is sought and the ground alleged for such
removal. The clerk shall thereupon deliver to the elector making the affidavit copies of petition papers for
demanding such a removal, printed copies of which he
shall keep on file for distribution as herein provided.
In issuing any such petition paper, the clerk shall enter
in a record to be kept in his office the name of the
elector to whom issued and the date of issuance, and the
number of the papers issued, and shall certify upon each
such paper the name of the elector to whom issued and
the date of issuance. No petition paper shall be accepted as part of a petition unless it bears such certificate of the clerk and unless filed as hereinafter provided. . . .

/Provisions are provided for filing of
petitions and elections./

SEC. 19.   Recall, Separate Petitions Required.

The question of recalling the mayor and any number
of members of the council may be submitted at the same
election, but as to each person whose removal is sought
a separate petition shall be filed and provision shall
be made for an entirely separate ballot. . . .

SEC. 21.   Result of Recall Election.

If a majority of the votes cast on the question of
recalling a member of the council or mayor shall be a-
gainst his recall he shall continue in office for the remainder of his unexpired term, but subject to recall as
before. If a majority of such votes be for the recall
of the member indicated on the ballots he shall, regard-
less of any defect in the recall petition, be deemed removed from office by recall, council shall immediately
provide for the nomination and election of his successor
for the unexpired term by fixing the time of the elections. The nomination and election of a person to succeed
a person so removed shall be held within one hundred and
twenty days after the date of the recall election and
shall be conducted in the same manner as provided for
regular municipal elections.

SEC. 22. Election When Member Resigns.

If the mayor or a member of the council in regard to
whom a recall petition is submitted to the council shall
resign within five days after notice thereof, the successor for the unexpired term shall be nominated and elected
as hereinbefore provided and the recall election shall

not be held.
SEC. 23.   Limitations on Recall Petitions.
No recall petition shall be filed against the mayor
or a member of the council within three months after he
takes office nor, in case of a person subjected to a
recall election and not removed thereby, until at least
six months after that election. . . .

CHAPTER 5

THE COUNCIL

SEC. 24.   Powers. Terms, Vacancies.
The legislative powers of the city except as reserved to the people by this charter, shall be vested in
a council, each member of which shall be elected from a
separate ward.   Members of council shall be elected for
a term of two years and shall serve until their successors are chosen and have qualified.   If at any time, the
office of a member of council is vacant by reason of non-
election, death, resignation, removal of residence from
the ward represented or from any other cause whatsoever,
except when the vacancy is caused by a recall petition,
such vacancy shall be filled by the council for the unexpired term.
SEC. 25.   Redividing the City Into Wards.
The council not later than December 31, 1946, and
thereafter immediately after the proclamation by the secretary of state stating the population of the cities of
Ohio, as determined by the federal census decennially
taken, shall redivide the city into 33 wards.   Wards so
formed shall be as nearly equal in population as may be,
composed of contiguous and compact territory, and bounded
by natural boundaries or street lines.   When any territory is annexed to the city the council shall by ordinances declare it a part of the adjacent ward or wards.
The division of the city into wards existing at the time
of the adoption of this amendment, shall continue until
changed by the council as provided herein.
SEC. 26.   Qualifications of Members of the Council.
Members of the council shall be residents of the city and have the qualifications of electors therein.   A
member of the council, who at the time of his election,
was a resident of the ward which he represents shall for-
feit his office if he removes therefrom.   Members of
council shall not hold any other public office or employment, except that of notary public or member of the state
militia, and shall not be interested in the profits or
emoluments of any contract, job, work or service in the
municipality.   Any member who shall cease to possess any
of the qualifications herein required shall forthwith for-
feit his office, and any such contract in which any member is or may become involved by the council.   No member

of the council shall, except in so far as is necessary in the performance of the duties of his office, directly or indirectly interfere in the conduct of the administrative department, or directly or indirectly take any part in the appointment, promotion or dismissal of any officer, or employee in the service of the city other than the officers or employees of the council.

SEC. 27. Salary and Attendance of Members of the Council.

The salaries of the members of the council first elected under this charter shall be fixed by the outgoing council. Thereafter the council may, by ordinance passed in any even numbered year, change the salary of members of the council thereafter elected. Until the salaries of the members of the council are fixed as provided in this section the salary of a member of the council shall be eighteen hundred ($1,800.00) dollars per year. . . . The Council may by ordinance provide compensation for its president in addition to that which he receives as a member of the council.

For each absence of a member from regular meetings of the council, unless authorized by a two-thirds vote of all members thereof, there shall be deducted a sum equal to two per cent (2%) of the annual salary of each member. Absence from ten (10) consecutive regular meetings shall operate to vacate the seat of a member unless such absence be authorized by the council.

* * *

SEC. 29. Rules of Council.

The Council shall determine its own rules and order of business and shall keep a journal of its proceedings. It may punish or expel any member for disorderly conduct or violation of its rules. No expulsion shall take place without the concurrence of two-thirds of all the members elected nor until the delinquent member shall have been notified of the charge against him and been given an opportunity to be heard.

SEC. 30. President of the Council.

At the first meeting in January following a regular municipal election, the council shall elect one of its members president who shall preside at meetings of the council and perform such duties as presiding officer as may be imposed upon him by the council. . . .

CHAPTER 11

THE EXECUTIVE

SEC. 67. Executive and Administrative Powers.

The executive and administrative powers of the city shall be vested in the mayor, directors of departments and other administrative officers provided for in this charter or by ordinance.

SEC. 68.   Terms and Qualifications of Mayor.

The mayor shall be the chief executive officer of
the city.   Except as otherwise in this charter provided, he
he shall be elected for a term of two years, assume office
on the first Monday following his election and serve until
his successor is elected and qualified.   The mayor shall
be an elector of the city and shall not hold any other
public office or employment, except that of notary public
or member of the state militia, and shall not be interested in the profits or emoluments of any contract, job,
work or service for the municipality.

SEC. 69. Salary of Mayor.

The salary of the mayor shall be fifteen thousand
dollars ($15,000.00) per annum, payable in twelve equal
monthly installments.

SEC. 70. Mayor's Appointing Power.

The mayor shall have power to appoint and remove directors of all departments, and officers and members of
commissions not included within regular departments.
Officers appointed by the mayor shall serve until removed
by him or until their successors are appointed and qualified.

SEC. 71. General Powers and Duties of Mayor.

It shall be the duty of the mayor to act as chief
conservator of the peace within the city; to supervise
the administration of the affairs of the city; to see that
all ordinances of the city are enforced; to recommend to
the council for adoption such measures as he may deem
necessary or expedient; to keep the council advised of
the financial condition and future needs of the city;
to prepare and submit to the council such reports as may
be required by that body, and to exercise such powers and
perform such duties as are conferred or required by this
charter or by the laws of the state.

SEC. 72. Mayor's Right in Council.

The mayor and the directors of all departments established by the charter, or that may hereafter be established by ordinance, shall be entitled to seats in the
council.   Neither the mayor nor the director of any department shall have a vote in the council, but the mayor
shall have the right to introduce ordinances and to take
part in the discussion of all matters coming before the
council; and the directors of departments shall be entitled to take part in all discussions of the council relating to their respective departments.   The council by ordinance or resolution may authorize other city officials
to have seats in council.

SEC. 73. Vacancy in the Office of Mayor--Acting
Mayor.

If at any time, which is more than one year before
the next regular municipal election, the office of mayor
is vacant by reason of non-election, death, resignation,
removal from office in any way except by recall election,

removal of residence from the city, or from any other
cause whatsoever, such vacancy shall be filled by special municipal elections. If at the time this section
takes effect, no eligible person has been elected to the
office of mayor in the manner provided in this charter,
then the office of mayor shall be deemed vacant by reason
of non-election. The aforesaid special municipal elections shall be held on the first Tuesday after sixty days
from the day on which said vacancy first occurs, at which
said vacancy first occurs, at which time the non-partisan
primary election shall be held, and on the fifth Tuesday
following the said non-partisan primary election, at
which time the final special municipal election shall be
held, and all the provisions in this charter contained as
to nomination and election of candidates for mayor at
regular municipal elections shall apply to the said special municipal elections. The person so elected as mayor
at the said special municipal elections shall assume the
office immediately upon his election and qualification and
shall serve until the first Monday following the next
regular municipal election and until his successor is
elected and qualified. During the existence of such vacancy in the office of mayor, pending the time the said
vacancy is filled by special municipal elections, the duties of the office of mayor shall be discharged by the
head of one of the departments provided for in this charter under the title of acting mayor; provided, however,
that if the vacancy occurs at a time when special municipal elections are not authorized in this section, then
the said head of one of the departments shall succeed to
the office of mayor and be mayor until the first Monday
after the next regular municipal election and until his
successor is elected and qualified. In either of the
above cases the order of succession as acting mayor or as
mayor shall be as follows: Director of law, director of
finance and director of public utilities. In all cases
at the next regular municipal election a mayor shall be
elected for the term of two years. If the mayor, or the
person performing the duties of mayor under the title
acting mayor, be temporarily absent from the city, or become temporarily disabled from any cause, his duties
shall be performed during such absence or disability by
the head of one of the aforesaid departments in the above
order, and under the title of acting mayor.

SEC. 74. Residence Requirement, Officers and Employees.

Except as in this charter otherwise provided or as
council may specially otherwise provide, every officer and
employee of the city of Cleveland must be a resident of
Cleveland.

SEC. 75. City Record.

The city shall publish weekly a City Record which
shall contain the transactions and proceedings of the

council, the legal advertising of the city and such other
information relating to the affairs of the city as shall
be determined by ordinance. The City Record shall be
published, distributed and sold in such manner and on
such terms as the council may determine. No unofficial
advertisements shall be published in the City Record.

SEC. 76. City Planning Commission.

There shall be a city planning commission composed
of seven (7) members. One shall be a member of the council of the City of Cleveland chosen by each council to
serve during the term of such council, and six members
shall be appointed by the mayor, and may be removed by
him. The term of the members, other than the council
member, shall be six (6) years, except that of the initial appointments, the terms of two members shall be two
(2) years and the terms of two members shall be four (4)
years. Vacancies in the commission shall be filled in
the same manner for the unexpired term. The chairman
of the commission shall be appointed annually by the mayor
from the members and may be removed as chairman at his
pleasure.

SEC. 76-1 Directors and Staff.

There shall be a planning director who shall be nominated by the commission and appointed by the mayor at
his discretion. He shall be ex-officio secretary of the
city planning commission and shall serve until removed
by the mayor with the concurrence of a majority of the
commission. Upon nomination of the planning director the
commission shall appoint as its staff such technical and
office personnel and assistants as it may deem necessary
within the appropriation made available for such purpose.
All such appointments, except the planning director and
his secretary, shall be made in conformity with the civil
service provisions of this charter. Under the direction
of the commission the director shall supervise and control
the planning staff.

SEC. 76-2. Powers and Duties of Commission.

It shall be the function and duty of the planning
commission to make and adopt a general plan for the development and improvement of the city, and for any area
outside of the city which in the judgment of the commission bears relation to the planning of the city. No
general plan or portions thereof or amendments thereto
shall be adopted by the commission until after a public
hearing thereon. So much of the general plan as may be
established or from time to time amended by ordinance of
council shall constitute the official map of the City of
Cleveland. The commission shall also make plans and proposals for specific improvements and projects which it
deems desirable for the city and its surrounding area and
recommend them to the appropriate authority. These plans
and proposals shall not become a part of the general plan
until adopted as such. The commission shall have authori-

ty to call upon officers and employees of other departments and divisions of the City of Cleveland for assist-
ance in city planning. On or before the 1st day of June
in each year the commission shall recommend to the mayor
a capital improvement budget for the following year and a
comprehensive five-year capital improvement program. It
shall be the duty of the commission to take the initiative in planning for the city and surrounding area and
it shall have full power to publish and distribute at
public expense copies of plans or reports and to promote
public interest in and understanding of general plans
and of other recommendations or proposals. It shall have
authority to make such investigations, maps and studies
relating to the planning of the community as it may deem
desirable. The planning commission may recommend to the
appropriate public authorities or private agencies pro-
grams for the development and improvement of the community, for the enactment of legislation pertaining thereto,
for the building of public structures and improvements
and for the financing thereof. The commission may enter
into agreement with other governmental or private agencies necessary or desirable for carrying forward any
of its purposes subject to the approval of council. . . .

CALL FOR REESTABLISHMENT OF THE CITY MANAGER PLAN
January 26, 1935

>The financial straits in which
>Cleveland found itself, led Mayor
>Harry Davis to call for a new bond
>issue to help meet additional costs
>of city government. Council Presi-
>dent Alexander De Maioribus accused
>the Mayor of excessive spending and
>fiscal mismanagement. He called
>for reestablishment of the City Ma-
>nagement Form of Government. The
>description of the issues raised,
>taken from the New York Times,
>indicates the problems involved.

Source: New York Times, January 27, 1935, Section II,
4:2.

CITY MANAGER PLAN UP IN CLEVELAND

A charter amendment calling for the restoration of
the city manager form of government in Cleveland will be
introduced in the City Council Monday night by Alexander
L. De Maioribus, Council president, and, if no corrections in the draft are necessary, the amendment will be
referred immediately to the Council's legislative assembly for hearings.

The De Maioribus ordinance, providing for a vote
by the people on the question of re-establishing the city
manager plan, would give the Council the alternative of
providing in the amendment for either the proportional
representation system of electing Councilmen or a method
under which a stipulated number of candidates for the
Council receiving the highest number of votes would be
elected.

Under the proportional representation system of voting, a citizen is permitted to vote for a first, second,
third, fourth, &c., choice for Council. A quota of first
choice ballots is arrived at for each district and candidates receiving votes in excess of the quota are elected.

If one or more of the candidates in a district fails
to reach the quota, the candidate receiving the least
number of first-choice ballots in the district is eliminated and second choices on his ballots are distributed
among the remaining candidates for whom they are marked.
This practice is continued until the successful candidates are determined.

Favors "Straight Vote" Method

Originally Mr. De Maioribus intended that the "straight vote" method should be provided in the amendment, but he later decided that the proportional representation system, which prevailed under Cleveland's previous manager plan, should be listed as an alternative.

The De Maioribus ordinance provides that the Council, which would select the city manager, should be elected from four districts, as was the case in the manager form of government Cleveland had from 1924 to 1932.

The Council would be composed of seventeen members, instead of twenty-five as under the old city manager charter or thirty-three as is now the case.

Mr. De Maioribus had said that if Council refuses to place his proposed amendment on the ballot he would circulate petitions, which, if sufficient signatures are obtained will make it mandatory that the measure be submitted to a vote of the electorate.

The Council president said his decision to fight for the return of the city manager plan of government is motivated by the fact that Cleveland's government "slipped back twenty-five years" when it adopted the present Mayor-Ward Council plan.

Councilmen Assail Mayor

The city's present Mayor, Harry L. Davis, has been bitterly attacked by members of the City Council, many of whom accuse him of being partly responsible for the city's present financial plight.

When the Mayor and his finance director went to Columbus to seek financial aid from the State Legislature, members of that body called him the "biggest spender" in the State.

Cleveland, which has defaulted both principal and interest on its bonded indebtedness, is now endeavoring to get the electorate to approve two more bond issues at special elections.

A special election will be held early next month, at which county voters will be asked to approve a welfare levy, tentatively set at 3.2 mills. At the same election or a little later in the year voters will be asked to approve a $6,000,000 deficiency bond issue, proceeds of which the city hopes to use for operating expenses.

Mayor Davis, according to Mr. De Maioribus, has issued $17,000,000 in deficiency bonds in his three terms as Mayor of the city.

At the present time Cleveland's bonded debt has reached the total of $117,144,722.

CITY MANAGEMENT AND CONTROL OF
THE CLEVELAND TRANSIT SYSTEM, 1943

> The city purchased the transit sys-
> tem on April 28, 1942. The pre-
> face of K. H. Ledford, secretary
> of the Cleveland Transit Board, in-
> dicates how the city established
> control. The excerpt from the City
> Charter illustrates how the Transit
> Board was established as well as
> its duties.

Source: <u>Charter of the City of Cleveland (as Amended)</u>
<u>With Separate Excerpt Relating to Operation, Management</u>
<u>and Control of the Cleveland Transit System</u>. Cleveland,
March 1944, 4-7.

Preface

On April 28, 1942, after lengthy negotiations, the
City of Cleveland purchased the assets and properties of
The Cleveland Railway Company, which operated a local
mass transportation system throughout the metropolitan
area.

Upon purchase of the transportation system by the
city, operation and management thereof became a part of
the activities of the Cleveland Department of Public U-
tilities, then already composed of a waterworks system,
electric light plant, steam heating plant, and sewage
treatment and disposal plants. The transportation system
became a division of said department, known as the "Division of Municipal Transportation," headed by a commis-
sioner, who was responsible to the director of the department.

It was recognized early that the mass transportation
system could not be efficiently managed and operated in
the same manner as were other publicly owned utilities.
In fact, the ordinance authorizing the issuance of re-
venue bonds for the purchase of the system by the city
contained a provision wherein it was declared to be the
intention of City Council to submit to the electorate
within one (1) year from the date of the bonds an amendment to the City Charter proposing to place the operation of the transportation system under a commission or
a board.

Pursuant to such provision, an ordinance was passed
by City Council on September 2, 1942, proposing an amendment to the City Charter, by providing for the management, supervision, and control of the transit facilities
of the city under the control of a Transit Board. The
charter amendment was submitted to the electorate, and
on November 3, 1942, was approved. Thus the Cleveland

Transit Board was established, effective January 1, 1943.
The provisions of the charter amendment are first
shown herein, followed by all other provisions of the
Charter of the City of Cleveland.

K. H. LEDFORD
Secretary, Cleveland Transit Board.

Excerpt from the Charter of the City of Cleveland,
Relating to the Operation, Management and
Control of the Cleveland Transit System.

Separate Control.
Section 113-1. It is hereby declared to be the con-
trolling legislative intent of the electors of the city
of Cleveland to provide for the supervision, management
and control of a board, as provided in Section 113-2.
The provisions contained in Sections 113-2 to 113-7, inclusive, and Section 142-1, shall be deemed exceptions
to any and all provisions in this charter inconsistent
with such purpose and intent. Every provision of this
charter governing administrative departments generally,
which conflicts with such supervision, management and control of the Cleveland Transit System, as provided in
Sections 113-1 to 113-8, inclusive, is to the extent of
such conflict only, hereby repealed.

Transit Board.
Section 113-2. There shall be a board composed of
three members appointed by the mayor, with the approval
of council, for overlapping six-year terms; provided that
the initial appointments shall be for terms commencing
Jan. 1, 1943, and of such initial appointments one shall
be for two years and one for four years. Appointments
after the initial appointment shall be for a full term
provided that any vacancy in the membership of the
board shall be filled for the balance of the unexpired
term in the same manner as original appointments. The
mayor shall designate the chairman of the board, who
shall serve as such at the pleasure of the mayor. The
chairman of the board shall be entitled to a seat in
council but not to a vote. Members of the board shall
not hold any other public office or employment except
that of notary public or member of the state militia, and
shall not be interested financially in the profits or
emoluments of any contract job, work or service for the
city nor have any financial or other interest in any public utility. Not more than two members shall belong to
the same political party. A member of the board may be
removed by the mayor but only after opportunity has been
afforded for a public hearing before the mayor within
ten (10) days after written charges have been given such
member by the mayor and a copy filed with the clerk of

council. Such member shall be heard in person or by
counsel and action of the mayor shall be final unless
not later than the second meeting of council thereafter,
the council shall disapprove such removal by the affirmative vote of two-thirds of the members elected thereto.
Notwithstanding the provisions of Section 191 each member shall be paid a uniform salary to be fixed by council
at not less than four thousand five hundred dollars
($4500.00) per year and not more than seven thousand dol-
lars ($7000.00) per year, except that the chairman, shall
be entitled to an additional five hundred dollars
($500.00) per year. All such salaries shall be paid
semi-monthly.

Duties of the Board.
     Section 113-3. The board shall meet immediately
after its appointment and proceed to organize and adopt
rules. Thereafter the board shall hold regular meetings
at least once each week at a time and place to be established as part of its rules and regulations. Special
meetings may be held at the call of the chairman, or at
the request of any two members. The board shall appoint
a general manager for the transit system who shall serve
at the pleasure of the board and who shall be in the un-
classified service. All meetings of the board shall be
open to the public and the board shall keep full and
accurate minutes of its proceedings and an abstract of
its proceedings shall be printed each week in the City
Record. The board shall act by resolution and a concurrence of two members appointed to the board shall be
sufficient for action by the board unless a different
number be required as otherwise provided in this charter.
     Subject to the general provisions of this charter,
except as modified with reference to the board and the
specific provisions in this and the next succeeding sections limiting such power, the board shall have full and
complete supervision, management and control of the transit system, both within and without the city limits, including the operation, maintenance and construction of
the system, a determination of routes, types of rolling
stock and equipment, time schedules and stops, the operation of cars, buses and other equipment, and the fixing
of the salary or compensation of its employees. The
board shall have no power or right to acquire by purchase,
lease or otherwise any transportation system, or any
part thereof, without the consent of council by ordinance,
passed not as an emergency measure, nor shall the board
have the right or authority to dispose of any of the
property or capital assets of the transit system without
similar consent of council. The board shall take no action concerning any permit, franchise, extension or renewal thereof, or other right to operate the transit system within the territorial limits of any other municipal-

ity or governmental subdivision unless such right to o-
perate has been first accepted by ordinance of council.
No new capital expenditure shall be made except with the
approval of council.

The board shall annually cause to be made and printed for public information and distribution a report, copies of which shall be furnished to the mayor and members of council, which may be in a condensed form showing
the financial results of city ownership and operation.
The board shall prepare for submission to the council,
at its second meeting of each month, a summary statement
of revenues and expenses for the preceding month detailed
as to operations and funds, in such manner as to show the
exact financial condition of the transit system operation
as of the last day of the preceding month. . . .

Separate Merit System for Transit Employees Only

Employees of Transit System.

Section 142-1. As an exception to the foregoing
civil service provisions and notwithstanding any provision in this charter contained to the contrary, appointments and promotions in the Cleveland Transit System shall
be made by the transit board, as and when established by
amendment to this charter, according to merit and fitness,
to be ascertained, as far as practicable, by competitive
examination. The transit board shall make rules and regulations for the enforcement of this provision and shall
establish by rule the seniority provisions relating to
street railway employees in effect at the time of the
acquisition of the transit system by the city of Cleveland. Notwithstanding anything in Section 191 or elsewhere in this charter contained, the salary or compensation of employees of the transit system shall be in accordance with the prevailing rates of salary or compensation for services rendered under similar conditions
of employment and of vacation, sick leave and retirement
privileges for like employment in the industry generally
and without reference to other departments or divisions
of the city of Cleveland. . . .

DEVELOPMENT OF THE UNIVERSITY CIRCLE AREA
March 21, 1964

> City planning had become essential
> in the post World War II era.
> Cleveland's plans had been care-
> fully pursued, and they surpassed
> their original goals. The twenty-
> year development program had pro-
> ceeded at such a rapid pace that
> it might be completed within ele-
> ven years. The basic issues are
> discussed in the selection below.

Source: New York Times, March 22, 1964, section VIII,
10:3.

An unusual cooperative plan for redeveloping the University Circle area of Cleveland will end its sixth year
of operation far ahead of schedule.
Conceived as a 20-year development involving the in-
vestment of $175 million, the University Circle program
is likely to reach its goal after 10 to 11 years of
operation.
Neil J. Carothers, president of the University Circle Foundation, reported that new structures worth $70
million were completed and that construction values at
$30 million was under way.

Backed by Church Groups
"We won't be able to maintain this pace," Mr. Carothers said, "but, at the rate we've been going, we may
complete the original plans in 11 years."
The University Circle program is supported by 30 organizations and agencies in an area of a square mile,
four miles east of downtown Cleveland. In 1957, these
groups formed the foundation and hired the planning firm
of Messrs. Howard and Greeley to draw a 20-year development project.
The best known of the sponsoring groups are Western
Reserve University, Case Institute of Technology, University Hospitals, the Cleveland Art Museum, the Cleveland
Orchestra, Art Institute of Cleveland, Western Reserve
Historical Society, Cleveland Institute of Music and the
Natural Science Museum.

Original Plans Enforced
In addition, the foundation is supported by seven
religious institutions representing all major faiths, a
group of welfare agencies, libraries and garden groups
in the area.
The foundation was created through donations of $3
million by a group of wealthy Clevelanders interested in

building an educational, cultural and medical center
for the community. A public drive netted $6 million
more.

The final money to operate the foundation came from
an unexpected bequest of $2.5 million from the estate of
Mrs. Andrew R. Jennings, a widow who had watched the development start from her apartment in nearby Wade Parl
Manor.

The foundation buys all real estate for member institutions and enforces adherence to the original master
plan. It also acquires and operates parking facilities
and employs a special police force of 19 men.

Law Was Amended

In cooperation with the University of Chicago, the
foundation won an amendment to the Federal housing law,
allowing educational institutions to participate in urban
renewal projects.

This law has helped University Circle to buy property along its border, protecting it from the spread of an
adjacent slum neighborhood.

The development has resulted in new buildings for
the Natural History Museum, Institutes of Music and Art,
Day Nursery and Maternal Health Association, a new Veterans Administration Mental Hospital and major additions
to the Art Museum, Historical Society, and the Cleveland
Hearing and Speech Center.

Western Reserve and Case Institute of Technology
have been the biggest beneficiaries. They have been able
to add new classrooms, laboratories and dormitories and
to break out of their tightly confined borders.

CLEVELAND SNIPERS, July 23-25, 1968

> After a period of calm in Cleveland
> following Mayor Carl Stokes' elec-
> tion, some tensions began to devel-
> op. Several snipers fired on po-
> licemen. As a result Governor
> James A. Rhodes ordered National
> Guardsmen into the City to restore
> peace. The description below il-
> lustrates problems faced by the
> administration, police and Guards-
> men as well as the attitudes of the
> people.

Source: New York Times, July 24, 1968, 1:1, July 25,
1968, 1:4-5, and July 26, 1968, 1:4.

The police used Brink's armored cars last night to
seal off an East Side Negro area after eight persons
were killed--three of them policemen hit by bursts of
automatic gunfire from snipers in an apartment building.
Two of the five civilians killed were snipers, the police
said. . . .
     As reinforcements rushed in, disturbances broke out
sporadically in other nearby areas.
     Gov. James A. Rhodes ordered all 15,250 Ohio National
Guardsmen to duty and said that 700 guardsmen in summer
training at Camp Perry, Ohio, would be sent to Cleveland.
. . .
     Last night's shooting was the first serious racial
flareup here since Mr. Stokes began his campaign for
Mayor more than a year ago.
     Last summer there were reports that the word was out
in Cleveland's black communities to "cool it for Carl"
while he was making a successful bid to become the first
elected Negro mayor of a major United States city.
     Cleveland has more than 300,000 Negro residents out
of a total population of 800,000.
     Three policemen were pinned down by gunfire and
pulled to safety about 1½ hours later as officers returned
heavy fire into a brick apartment building on Lakeview
Road and tried to help the wounded officers.
     The area was blocked off. . . .
     Mr. Stokes asked all radio stations in the city to
broadcast that people in the area "should cooperate with
the police."
     "We definitely need the help of all citizens," he
said. . . .

Negro Patrol Ordered in Cleveland Slums
New York Times, July 25, 1968

Mayor Carl B. Stokes ordered all National Guard troop
troops and white policemen withdrawn yesterday from a
six-square mile area on this city's troubled East Side.
* * *
The area was placed under the control of 125 Negro
police officers and Negro Cuyahoga County sheriff's
deputies, the Negro Mayor announced at a news conference
yesterday afternoon. . . .
All liquor stores and taverns were closed for 72
hours. . . .
General Del Corso said he had recommended against
withdrawing troops from the area but went along with the
Mayor's idea of replacing them with black policemen and
community workers. . . .

Cleveland Mayor Sends Guard Back to Patrol Slums
New York Times, July 26, 1968.

Mayor Carl B. Stokes ordered the police and National
Guardsmen to return to the East Side tonight /July 25/.
He abandoned the Negro citizens' patrols he had established in the area after an outbreak of looting.
He also announced a 9 P.M.-to-6 A.M. curfew in the
area and told residents to obey the orders of the police
and guardsmen. . . .
In a radio and television message to the people of
the city /Mayor Stokes/ said:
". . . I am having the National Guard troops in the
stores which have been broken into and looted. They will
be guarded in protection of property. In regard to re-
moving the last vestige of shame from the Negro community,
it's going to be necessary that each and every black citizen in this city help in that regard. Part of that
means that you stay off the streets yourself, but more
importantly, that you keep the young off the streets.
. . ."
There are 3,100 National Guardsmen in the city now,
about 400 of whom are in the Negro area. In the most
sensitive sections the police are using patrol cars with
integrated crews. . . .

BIBLIOGRAPHY

The works cited have been carefully selected to indicate the major
sources to be consulted for further
research on the growth and development of Cleveland. Materials listed
have been published during the nineteenth and twentieth centuries. The
variety of works was chosen to provide a cross-section of the information on the social, economic and
political life of the city. Students should also consult the Rea-
der's Guide to Periodical Litera-
ture, and Social Science and Huma-
nities Index for further articles
on Cleveland.

PRIMARY SOURCES

The Acts to Provide for the Organization of Cities and
    Villages and the Revised Ordinances of the City of
    Cleveland; With the Ordinances Establishing Streets
    and Their Grades. Cleveland, 1855.

An Analysis of a Slum Area in Cleveland, Prepared for
    Cleveland Metropolitan Housing Authority. . .
    Cleveland, 1934.

The Annual Report of the Cleveland Board of Zoning Ap-
    peals. No. 1- . 1929/30 -. Cleveland, 1931 -
    date.

Annual Report of the Water Works Trustees. . . for the
    Year Ending December 31. Cleveland, 1857-1914.

The Charter and the Codified Ordinances of the City of
    Cleveland. Cleveland, 1951.

Charter of the City of Cleveland, Ohio (as amended). With
    Separate Excerpt Relating to Operation, Management
    and Control of the Cleveland Transit System. Cleve-
    land, 1944.

Charters of the Village of Cleveland, and the City of
    Cleveland With Their Several Amendments; to Which
    Are Added the Laws and Ordinances of the City of
    Cleveland. Cleveland, 1851.

Cleveland. The City Record. vol. 1 - date. 1914 -
      date. Cleveland, 1914 - date.

Cleveland. Charter Commission. Journal of the First
      Charter Commission of Cleveland. Cleveland, 1913.

Cleveland. Citizen's Committee. Report . . . Cleve-
      land's Financial Problem and Suggestive Measures
      of Relief. Cleveland, 1919.

Cleveland Automobile Club. . . . Report on Traffic Sys-
      tem for Cleveland Based on Studies Made in Eight
      Cities. Cleveland, 1925.

Cleveland City Council. Manual. Cleveland, 1891-1901.

---------------------. Proceedings. 1868/9 - 1921/22.
      Also in City Record. Cleveland, 1877-1923.

---------------------. Inauguration of the Perry Statue,
      at Cleveland, on the Tenth of September, 1860; In-
      cluding the Addresses at Other Proceedings, With a
      Sketch of William Walcutt the Sculptor. Cleveland,
      1861.

Cleveland. City. City Manager Plan Commission. Report.

Cleveland. City Planning Commission. . . . Annual Six
      Year Capital Improvement Program. Cleveland, 1947-
      50.

-----------------------------------. Cleveland Today,
      Tomorrow; The General Plan of Cleveland. Cleveland,
      1950.

-----------------------------------. The Cleveland
      Thorofare Plan. City of Cleveland. Cleveland,
      1921.

-----------------------------------. Looking Ahead for
      the Goodrich Area Report. Cleveland, 1956.

-----------------------------------. Lorain-Carnegie
      Bridge and River Improvement. Cleveland, 1926.

-----------------------------------. Our Downtown Park-
      ing Headache and How We Can Cure It. Cleveland
      Downtown Parking Survey, Preliminary Report. Cleve-
      land, 1951.

-----------------------------------. Planning Cleve-
      land . . . Report. 1929 - 1945.

Cleveland. Civil Service Commission. Annual Report.
     1910 - 1950. Cleveland, 1911 - 1951.

-------------------------------------. Rules and Regula-
     tions . . . and Provisions of the Charter of the
     City of Cleveland Covering the Civil Service Com-
     mission. Cleveland, 1914.

Cleveland. Mayor's Advisory War Committee. Cleveland
     in the War. A Review of Work Accomplished by the
     Mayor's Advisory War Committee and Work Proposed
     During the Great Period of Reconstruction. Cleve-
     land, 1919.

Celeveland. Educational Research Bureau. Occupational
     Information Series, nos. 1-5. Cleveland, 1929-
     1930.

Cleveland, City Education Board. The All Year School
     Plan in Cleveland. An Explanation of the Proposed
     System and What It Is Designed to Accomplish.
     Cleveland, 1910.

Cleveland. Education Board. Annual Report. 1854/55 -
     1943/44. Cleveland, 1855 - 1944. 1927/28 - 1937/38
     have title: Report. 1936/37, statistical data only;
     full report not published. Ceased publication
     1943/44.

--------------------------. The Cleveland Technical
     High School, Its Inception, Building and Equipment,
     Together with an Outline of the Course of Study.
     Cleveland, 1909.

--------------------------. Preliminary Report on Sim-
     plified Course of Study. Cleveland, 1909.

--------------------------. The Three R's. Improve-
     ment in Them, Place in Present Course of Study.
     Cleveland, 1909.

Cleveland. James Ford Rhodes High School. South Brook-
     lyn; A Brief History of that Part of the City of
     Cleveland Which Lies South of Big Creek and West of
     the Cuyahoga River. Cleveland, 1946.

Cleveland. Metropolitan Housing Authority. Annual Re-
     port. 1940 - present. Cleveland, 1940 - present.

Cleveland. Public Health and Welfare Depart, Charities
     and Corrections Division. Annual Report. Cleve-
     land, 1891 - 1915. 1891 - 1902 issued by the Chari-
     ties and Corrections Department. Division abolished.

Later reports on charities and corrections included
in the Annual Report of the Public Health and
Welfare Department.

--. Health
Division. Annual Report. Cleveland, 1872 - 1946.
1871/72 - 1913 issued by the Public Health and Sanitation Department. 1942 - 1944 not published.

Cleveland. Public Properties Department. Recreation
Division. Annual Report.

Cleveland. Public Safety Department, Fire Division.
Annual Report. 1864/65 - 1928-31. Cleveland,
1865 - 1932. 1915 - 1927 not published. Reports
for 1903 - 1914 included in the Annual Report of
the Public Safety Department. Police Division.
1864/65 - 1866/67 issued by the Fire Department;
1895 - 1902, by the Fire Department.

Cleveland. Public Safety Department. Police Division.
Annual Report. Issued by the Police Department
1876 - 1902 (as the Board of Police Commissioners,
1876-90). Not published 1915-25. The reports of
the Police Division and the Fire Division of the
Public Safety Department issued together as the
Annual Report of the Department, 1903 - 1914.

Cleveland. Public Service Department Division of Parks.
Annual Report. Cleveland, 1895 - 1916.

Cleveland. Public Utilities Department. Light and
Power Division. Annual Report. 1914 - present.
Cleveland, 1915 - present.

Cleveland. Public Utilities Department. Cleveland's
Municipally Owned Public Utilities; Water Supply,
Sewage Disposal /and/ Electric Light and Power . . .
Published to Acquaint the Citizens of Cleveland with
this large Industry of Which They Are Sole Heirs.
Cleveland.

Cleveland Rapid Transit Commissioners Board. Report on a
Rapid Transit System for the City of Cleveland Made
to the Board of Rapid Transit Commissioners, City
of Cleveland. New York, 1919.

Cleveland. Sesquicentennial Commission. The Year of
Celebration, 1946; A Report of the Cleveland Sesquicentennial. . . Cleveland, December 31, 1946.

Cleveland. Transit Board. A Modernization Plan for the
Cleveland Transit System. Cleveland, 1944.

Codified Ordinances of the City of Cleveland, Including
    all General Ordinances in Force March 1, 1877. To-
    gether With All Special Ordinances of Public In-
    terest. Cleveland, 1877.

Corre, Mary Price. The Metal Industries in Cleveland; A
    Vocational Study Prepared for the Cleveland Pub-
    lic Schools. Cleveland, 1924.

General Acts Relative to the Organization of Cities and
    Villages, the School Laws, Governing the City
    Schools in Force June 1, 1868, and the Revised Or-
    dinances of the City of Cleveland. . . October 25,
    1867   Cleveland, 1868.

General Ordinances of the City of Cleveland, in Force
    July 1, 1872. Cleveland, 1872.

High School Radio Workshops in Cleveland; A Survey by
    Radio Teachers and Station WBOE, Cleveland, Ohio,
    . . . Washington, D. C., 1957.

Joiner, David A., comp. Private Developments in Cleve-
    land's Urban Renewal Areas. Cleveland, 1957.

Municipal Code of the City of Cleveland in Force July
    1st, 1921. Including all Ordinances of a General
    Nature, the Charter. . . and all Amendments Thereto.
    Cleveland, 1921.

Municipal Law for the Government of Cleveland. . . 1891.
    Cleveland, 1891.

Official Programme of the Centennial Celebration of the
    Founding of the City of Cleveland and the Settlement
    of the Western Reserve. Cleveland, 1896.

Ordinances of the City of Cleveland. Containing all
    General and Specific Ordinances of Public Interest
    in Force July 10, 1882. Cleveland, 1882

Ordinances of the City of Cleveland. Containing all
    General and Specific Ordinances of Public Interest
    in Force May 19, 1890 and an Addenda to October 20,
    1890. Cleveland, 1890.

Ordinances of the City of Cleveland. Containing all
    General and Specific Ordinances of Public Interest
    in Force December 14th, 1896. Cleveland, 1897.

Ordinances of the City of Cleveland. Containing all
    General and Specific Ordinances of Public Interest
    in Force, January 1, 1907. Cleveland, 1907.

Proposed Charter for the City of Cleveland. Prepared
    and Proposed by the Charter Commission. Election
    day Tuesday, July 1, 1913.

Report of the Special Tax Commission of the City of
    Cleveland, Appointed by the Mayor at the Request
    of the City Council. Cleveland, 1915.

Report of the Cleveland Transit Board. 1942 - date.
    Cleveland, 1943 - present.

Schoenfeld, A. Raymond. Cleveland Downtown Parking Sur-
    vey: Final Report. Cleveland, 1952.

Stein, Herman D., ed. The Crisis in Welfare in Cleve-
    land; Report of the Mayor's Commission. Cleveland,
    1969.

United States Works Progress Administration. Ohio.
    Annals of Cleveland. Court Record Series. vols.
    1-10, 1837-1877. Cleveland, 1938-39.

--,
    Annals of Cleveland -- 1819-1935; A Digest and In-
    dex of the Newspaper Record of Events and Opinions
    in Two Hundred Volumes. Cleveland, 1936-38.

Whitter, Robert Harvey. The Cleveland Zone Plan. Report
    to the City Plan Commission Outlining Tentative Zone
    Plan for Cleveland. Cleveland, 1921.

                    SECONDARY SOURCES

Avery, Elroy McKendree. Cleveland in a Nutshell. An
    Historical and Descriptive Ready Reference Book.
    . . Cleveland, 1893.

----------------------. A History of Cleveland and Its
    Environs; The Heart of New Connecticut. Chicago
    and New York, 1918, 3 vols. This is a good detailed
    study of the development of Cleveland through the
    early 20th century.

Benton, Elbert Jay. Cultural Story of an American City,
    Cleveland. Cleveland, 1943-46, 3 vols. This is an
    interesting insight into the intellectual aspects
    of the city.

Burton, Clarence Monroe. A Chapter in the History of
    Cleveland. Detroit, 1895.

Chapman, Edmund H. Cleveland: Village to Metropolis;
    A Case Study of Problems of Urban Redevelopment in
    Nineteenth Century America. Cleveland, 1964.

Cleveland, Horace Gilette. An Account of the Lineage
    of General Moses Cleaveland of Canterbury . . .
    Connecticut, the Founder of the City of Cleveland,
    Ohio. . . Also a Sketch of His Life. . .   Cleve-
    land, 1885.

Cleveland, Past and Present; Its Representative Men: Com-
    prising Biographical Sketches of Pioneer Settlers
    and Prominent Citizens, With a History of the City,
    and Historical Sketches of Its Commerce, Manufac-
    turers. . . Cleveland, 1869.

Coates, William R. A History of Cuyahoga County and the
    City of Cleveland. Chicago and New York, 1924, 3
    vols. This is a good and valuable study of the
    city, its environs and its historical development.

Comley, William J. and W. d'Eggeville. Ohio: The Future
    Great State. Her Manufacturers and a History of
    Her Commercial Cities, Cincinnati and Cleveland, . .
    Cincinnati, 1875.

Cook, Huldah Florence. The Magyars of Cleveland; With a
    Brief Sketch of Their Historical Political and Social
    Backgrounds. Cleveland, 1919.

Coulter, Charles Wellesley. The Poles of Cleveland; With
    a Brief Sketch of Their Historical Political and
    Social Backgrounds. Cleveland, 1919.

Davison, Kenneth E. Cleveland During the Civil War. Co-
    lumbus, Ohio, 1962. This is a valuable study of the
    role played by the citizens and their leaders during
    the Civil War.

Freese, Andrew. Early History of the Cleveland Public
    Schools. Cleveland, 1876. This is interesting for
    the development of the school system and some as-
    pects of the philosophy of the time.

Hall, Theodore. The Sesquicentennial Story of Cleveland,
    1796-1946. Cleveland, 1946.

Johnson, Cristfield. History of Cuyahoga County, Ohio.
    . . General History of the County. . . History
    of Cleveland. . . History of the Townships. . .
    Cleveland, 1879.

Johnson, Tom Loftin. My Story. ed. by Elizabeth J.

Hauser. New York, 1911. This work is important
for its study of the times as told by the Mayor and
political leader of the city.

Kennedy, James Henry. A History of the City of Cleveland; Its Settlement, Rise and Progress, 1796-1896.
Cleveland, 1896. This is a fine detailed study of
the city and its first hundred years.

Ledbetter, Mrs. Eleanor E. The Czechs of Cleveland, With
a Brief Sketch of Their Historical and Political
Backgrounds. Cleveland, 1919.

------------------------. The Jugoslavs of Cleveland,
With a Brief Sketch of Their Historical and Political Backgrounds. Cleveland, 1918.

------------------------. The Slovaks of Cleveland,
With Some General Information on the Race. . .
Cleveland, 1918.

Lorenz, Carl. Tom L. Johnson, Mayor of Cleveland. New
York, 1911. A good account of this major political
leader.

Official Report of the Centennial Celebration of the
Founding of the City of Cleveland and the Settle-
ment of the Western Reserve. comp. by Edward A.
Roberts. Cleveland, 1896.

Orth, Samuel Peter. A History of Cleveland, Ohio. Chicago, 1910, 3 vols. This is a good historical study and biographical dictionary of some of the leading citizens. Much documentary material is presented.

Post, Charles Asa. Doans Corners and the City Four
Miles West. . . . Cleveland, 1930. This is an
interesting narrative of some of the major features
in the development of Cleveland.

Powell, Lyman Pierson, ed. Historic Towns of the Western
States. Section on Cleveland by C. F. Thwing. New
York, 1901. This is a summary of some of the de-
velopments in Cleveland.

Robison, W. Scott. History of the City of Cleveland; Its
Settlement, Rise and Progress. Cleveland, 1887.

Rose, William Ganson. Cleveland; the Making of a City.
Cleveland, 1950. This is a comprehensive chronology of the history of the city.

Uram, Clara A. Centennial History of Cleveland. Cleveland, 1896.

Wallen, James. Cleveland's Golden Story; A Chronicle of
Hearts That Hoped, Minds That Planned and Hands That
Toiled, To Make a City "Great and Glorious." After
data by Professor William M. Gregory. Cleveland,
1920. This is a sympathetic history of the city
indicating many of the major figures throughout its
growth.

Whittlesey, Charles. Early History of Cleveland, Ohio,
Including Original Papers and Other Matter Relating
to the Adjacent Country. With Biographical Notices
of the Pioneers and Surveyors. Cleveland, 1867.
This work presents much valuable documentary material
concerning the early history of the city.

Wickham, Gertrude van Rensselaer. The Pioneer Families
of Cleveland, 1796 - 1840. Cleveland, 1896, 2 vols.

Wilson, Ella (Grant). Famous Old Euclid Avenue of Cleveland, At One Time Called the Most Beautiful Street
in the World. Cleveland, 1932-37. 2 vols.

"The World's" History of Cleveland, Commemorating the
City's Centennial. . . Cleveland, 1896.

ARTICLES

Chadsey, M. "Cultural Centers and Hinterlands," Survey,
LX (September 15, 1928), 606-607.

Maxey, C. C. "Cleveland Revolts," National Municipal
Review. XI (January, 1922), 13-16.

Rumbold, C. "City Planning in Cleveland," National Municipal Review. XIX (October, 1930), 681-683.

Sham, N. "Cleveland's City Manager," National Municipal
Review. XIV (December, 1925), 715-721.